Struggle & Suffrage in Bradford

Struggle & Suffrage in Bradford

Women's Lives and the Fight for Equality

Rachel Bellerby

PEN & SWORD
HISTORY

AN IMPRINT OF PEN & SWORD BOOKS LTD.
YORKSHIRE – PHILADELPHIA

First published in Great Britain in 2019 by
Pen & Sword HISTORY
An imprint of
Pen & Sword Books Limited
Yorkshire - Philadelphia

ISBN 978 1 52671 6 927

A CIP catalogue record for this book is available from the British Library

Printed and bound in the UK
by TJ International Ltd, Padstow, Cornwall

Pen & Sword Books Limited incorporates the imprints of Atlas,
Archaeology, Aviation, Discovery, Family History, Fiction, History, Maritime,
Military, Military Classics, Politics, Select, Transport, True Crime, Air World,
Frontline Publishing, Leo Cooper, Remember When, Seaforth Publishing,
The Praetorian Press, Wharncliffe Local History, Wharncliffe Transport,
Wharncliffe True Crime and White Owl.

For a complete list of Pen & Sword titles please contact
PEN & SWORD BOOKS LIMITED
47 Church Street, Barnsley, South Yorkshire S70 2AS, United Kingdom
E-mail: enquiries@pen-and-sword.co.uk
Website: www.pen-and-sword.co.uk

Or
PEN AND SWORD BOOKS
1950 Lawrence Rd, Havertown, PA 19083, USA
E-mail: Uspen-and-sword@casematepublishers.com
Website: www.penandswordbooks.com

Contents

Acknowledgements

It would be almost impossible (and probably foolhardy) to write a book of local history stories without tapping into the knowledge of local people. During my time writing this book I've been lucky enough to work with and be inspired by some of Bradford's finest historians and storytellers. And, of course Bradford is home to several great libraries and archives that are staffed by people with a passion for the past.

Thanks are due to the following, and apologies for anyone I've missed: staff at Bradford Archives and Bradford Local Studies Libraries; members of Thornton Antiquarians, Heaton & District Local History Group, Bradford World War I Group, Saltaire History Group; researchers and historians Derek Barker, Helen Broadhead, Alan Cattell, Richard Coomber (Shipley in World War I website), Nigel Grizzard, Chris Power and Tricia Restorick. And lastly my dear friend and colleague Tina Jackson, who has been writing the Women of Leeds volume in this series and who kept me inspired and motivated.

Introduction

❖

When I began researching this book more than a year ago I began to wonder what I had let myself in for, since it seemed that the history of Bradford as we know it was very much dominated by men. The wool barons, politicians and entrepreneurs seemed largely to be male and I wondered whether my task would be fruitless.

But it soon became apparent that the women of the city do very much have tales to tell and it's been exciting to tease out the history of Bradford women from a variety of sources including newspapers, court reports, theatre programmes, official documents and photograph collections.

Of course, there's never been such a thing as a 'typical' Bradford woman, but by exploring different areas, classes and experiences we can begin to appreciate what life was like in Bradford during the century this book covers, from 1850 to 1950. Obviously, women didn't live their lives isolated from the men and children. The vast majority carried out a variety of roles in society including wife, mother, sister, daughter, employee, employer, club member, etc. Throughout the coming chapters, we'll explore what it meant to be a female during this exciting time, when so many changes were underway – both good and bad.

And so, after many an enjoyable day spent exploring libraries and archives, joining history walks around the city, and talking to women and men of Bradford, these tales are collected together to tell the story of 100 years of Bradford life as seen from the perspective of the city's female population. We'll meet merchants and mill-workers, philanthropists and philanderers, suffragettes and strikers.

Let us take a journey back across the centuries and find out what life was like in this marvellous city in years gone by.

CHAPTER ONE

Home Life

❖

A household at the start of our period, no matter how wealthy, would have relied on gas lighting or candlelight, with little in the way of labour-saving devices (although, of course, servants would assist those who could afford their services), and the only means of getting out and about was on foot, horseback or by coach. In contrast, by the start of the 1950s, electricity was in many homes, appliances such as fridges and vacuum cleaners were becoming commonplace, the TV revolution was just around the corner and car ownership was within the reach of many families.

Different experiences

In the nineteenth century, around eighty per cent of Bradford residents lived within a nuclear family, with a further ten per cent living with extended family. Lodgers were one way for a family to make money when extra funds were needed, and this type of arrangement was often a way that a widow could afford to stay in her house if she had the space for an extra occupant and was willing to cook and do laundry for the lodger.

Living conditions varied according to a woman's social class, her occupation (and that of her husband if applicable), and whether she was a wife, widow or daughter. These conditions also changed over time. The state of inner-city slums inhabited by newly-arrived immigrants in the mid-nineteenth century bore no resemblance whatsoever to the beautiful suburban homes of a 1950s' family living somewhere like Heaton or Baildon.

Nevertheless, there are some characteristics of home life in Bradford that made life in the city unique and, as such, are worth exploring. Firstly, the profusion of back-to-back housing for working-class people (which could also be found in other mill towns around Yorkshire, such as Leeds and Halifax) meant that close-knit communities were common. These streets were characterised by the corner shops at the end of every few rows of houses, by the crowds of workers walking to and from the workplace as the factory bell sounded, and by the various street sellers who hawked wares such as fruit & vegetables, pins & buttons and household goods from door-to-door.

Secondly, most people would have been able to see at least a few mill chimneys from their street or neighbourhood, whether that was the nearby mill where they or other family members worked (in which case their lives would have been punctuated by the sound of the mill buzzer and machinery) or a distant mill. Either way, Bradford folk were well aware of the town's position as a world leader in textiles during this time. Although there were periods of slump and recovery, the textile industry was a part of everyday life. People talked about the trade in shops, workplaces and in the street, and the state of the trade influenced life in town – a period of slump would affect shops and services not directly connected, as people would be spending less money.

Thirdly, the pollution emitted by the mill chimneys affected home life for thousands of families. Washing would become dirty when pegged outside, 'wheezy' children and adults would struggle to breathe, and seeing filthy smoke rise above the housetops was an everyday sight.

Sadly, infant mortality and disease were other factors affecting home life, which made Bradford unique for all the wrong reasons – the high rate of child deaths and the prevalence of disease, particularly in the early part of our period. With only thirty per cent of children born to textile workers reaching the age of 15 during the Industrial Revolution, either being part of a bereaved family or knowing a bereaved family would have been a sad and common fact of life.

Until the early twentieth century, childhood was short for working-class Bradfordians – either because of death and illness, or because children had to contribute to the family coffers from as early an age as possible, toiling in a shop or factory when they should have been playing outside.

What can we learn about the home lives of women during our period? Oral history is one way to get a snapshot of what life was like for Bradfordians of many different backgrounds. The collections of the Bradford Local Studies Library contain hundreds of interviews with both women and men about home life, some of which are explored in the following chapters. They recall local people working from home to earn money, such as making broth and bread for workers, or doing garment repairs or cobbling.

Housing

Bradford had (and still has) many different types of housing, ranging from one-room flats through to palatial villas on private roads. The city is noted for its back-to-back housing, which was particularly common in areas around textile mills. However, this type of housing had so many health risks that it was, for a time, banned. Ordinary terraced houses and back-to-backs were the typical dwellings of thousands of working-class families, and slums also existed in older buildings, with some families surviving in run-down and un-aired habitations shared with other families, with dozens of people using the same washing and toilet facilities. For most in these communities, the toilet facilities could be found in a lean-to building at the bottom of the yard – and it was the lucky ones who didn't have to share with other families. The expression 'I'm just going to t'back' would see the person in question go down the backyard and into the dark toilet, with newspapers pegged onto a nail in lieu of toilet paper.

And it wasn't just toilet facilities that could be found 'at the back'. Most working-class areas used the 'back lane' for leaving and entering the house, with the front door used only for visitors or special occasions. Street traders, such as the coalman and milkman, would bring their carts down the back lane and customers would go up to them that way.

In 1886, slums could still be found in areas such as Goitside (the streets behind what is now the Alhambra), about which one journalist wrote:

> There was not a single house in the row that had not two, three or more broken windows … a newspaper, an old coat or a straw hat is thrust into the gap.

Some of the first ever council housing was built in this area, as flats. In the years at the start of our period, cheap homes for the working-class were built, and age-old farmhouses were converted into terraced houses or back-to-backs. In each case, whether the building was new or old, a family with six children could quite possibly be living in just two rooms.

Unskilled workers generally lived in the back-to-back tunnel-houses, while large terraced properties were for skilled workers, such as artisans and teachers who wouldn't have had servants but maybe lodgers. Kathleen Binns, daughter of a worsted merchant, who lived in Athol Road, recalled that she went to a private school off Oak Lane run by a German lady:

> Life came to us rather than our venturing out to seek it … like … a German band marching along the road.

Despite the fact that Kathleen and her family might have seemed to outsiders to live a privileged life, the young girl remembered that her mother always seemed to be engaged in household tasks. The family had no servants.

The streets of terraced houses that characterise routes radiating from the city centre had a corner shop at the end of every few blocks, as well as a parade of shops within walking distance. For many women, these shops were a part of everyday social life and there were certain establishments that would offer 'tick' (free credit), allowing known customers to run up a tab before pay-day and then settle the bill once the wage came in.

The Co-operative stores were also popular, particularly for their dividend loyalty scheme where shoppers were given stamps whenever a purchase was made. When the book of stamps was completed, the customer could exchange it for goods in lieu of cash.

The next step up on the housing ladder was a semi-detached house, and if people improved their domestic circumstances, they were often able to move out to the suburbs and live on a wider street with more space inside the house and the added benefit and prestige of a front and back garden.

However, despite the lure of the suburbs, there were many areas, and Manningham is one of the best examples, where street after street of terraced houses existed alongside fine villas for wealthy people, which stood on private roads and included accommodation for live-in staff.

The larger villas were built with accommodation for servants, and local girls would have been employed here. For example, on the 1881 census, merchant Jacob Philipp is shown living at Clifton House with his son and four female servants – a housekeeper, cook, housemaid and servant. And close by at Clifton Villas lived a widow named Sarah Calvert with her two female servants. Belle Vue Place in Manningham was one of the finest addresses in the district and is still one of the best examples of a stylish terrace in Bradford.

Heaton Mount, built in 1863, was the first in the town to be glazed with plate-glass. When the Woolsorters' Gardens were sold two years later, work began to create new dwellings called 'freehold villa sites'. The large houses around the Oak Avenue area even had stables and coach-houses. However, by the 1860s, land was becoming difficult to find in Manningham and richer Bradfordians began to move further afield, to Calverley, Apperley Bridge and Baildon, with the railway providing the opportunity for residents to become some of the first rail commuters, coming in from Ilkley.

The houses of middle-class professionals would have had room for servants, reception rooms in which to receive guests, and often a separate space to allow a professional worker, such as a doctor or dentist, to work from his or her home premises. Many of these salubrious addresses were closed off by gates at the end of the plot, creating a private road and entirely separate from the surrounding working-class terraces. By the late 1800s, these types of houses would begin to be built with indoor bathrooms, many years before humbler homes were built with indoor facilities.

Extra money

During their lifetime, many working-class women would go through periods of being in paid employment and then, perhaps when the children were young, find a way to make money from home. Options included informal work such as carrying out dressmaking for neighbours, cleaning houses or taking in washing. Each of these was seen as a respectable way to earn money.

Less favoured by some was the process of pawning goods, something that many families would avoid, even in the direst need, for fear of the social backlash. Pawn shops made their money by taking in items from the person wanting to pawn goods and giving an agreed cash payment. The item could then be redeemed with interest after a set period of time or, if the person couldn't make the payment in time, the item was sold and the money went to the shop owner, along with any profit he or she was able to make.

Another way to borrow or make money was the practice of payment clubs, such as informal Christmas clubs where a group of women handed an agreed sum of money to a collector, who paid out just before Christmas and kept a small amount for herself. This was a good scheme for anyone not wanting to dip into their savings. When the clubs paid out, long queues formed outside the shops as local women waited to collect their turkey, vegetables, fruit and nuts.

Laundry, chores and keeping clean

The tasks of keeping the house clean, clothes well laundered and the house in good order, as well as doing the shopping, took up much more time than it would today. Today's labour-saving devices literally do save time and energy and no longer are people tied to daily shopping, thanks to almost universal access to a fridge and a freezer.

In the early days, there were women who paid servants to keep their home clean – who already carried out their own housework, perhaps with a little help from a maid or cleaner, and those who not only had to keep their own home clean but may have worked in someone else's home as a domestic help.

A working-class woman in a family living on an ordinary street of houses could be judged by her housekeeping, for example how often the front step was cleaned, how sparkling the windows and net curtains were, and whether, horror of horrors, the washing was hung out to dry on a Sunday.

Wash day could literally take up an entire day, usually a Monday, and could be done either in the home or at a laundry or washhouse. Often taking advantage of the time when the rest of the family were out at work or school, the woman of the house would do her washing and drying, and any meals provided that day would be a simple affair, such as fried-up leftovers from Sunday, or soup with bread and cheese. In a small house, washday could take over the whole of the downstairs, particularly in wet weather, with washing drying over the heads of everyone in the kitchen. The rooms filled with steam from the washing, and the mangle took up floor space.

Household chores were very much the preserve of women, with change happening very slowly. Right up until the 1960s and 1970s, female students learnt sewing and home economics at school, while their male counterparts did woodwork and mechanics. Even in those households where a woman went out to work, the expectation was still that she would carry out the household chores, perhaps with the help of a relative or the older children.

This sort of work would have been very much of the heavy variety, with rugs taken out to be beaten, bedding and other heavy materials pushed wet through the mangle, floors to mop, windows to clean and steps to scrub, often with little more than soap and water. By the mid-1950s, twin-tub washing machines were coming within the budget of domestic households. Yet even those lucky enough to buy such a machine couldn't simply leave it to do its job – you had to watch the tap while the machine filled and, once the clothes were washed, transfer them with wooden tongs to the rinse tub, several times depending on how many spins were needed.

Any large domestic appliance, such as a twin-tub, radio or refrigerator, could be bought on hire purchase with a deposit and then paid off in small weekly payments, often over a couple of years. The small adverts of local newspapers of the period are a great indication of what technology was available and at what price – with both new and second-hand items advertised. Over the years, emerging technology has been advertised, with stores inviting customers into their premises to see demonstrations of the likes of vacuum cleaners, radios, televisions, refrigerators and even electric blankets. All of the big Bradford department stores had electrical departments once electricity had reached domestic homes, and there were numerous independent electrical retailers.

In an era before central heating, the open fire was both a curse and a blessing, helping to keep the home warm yet also needing to be cleaned and laid each morning, and the soot and ashes disposed of. The fire was the heart of the home, used not only for warming the room but for drying clothes, boiling water, toasting bread and even burning small bits of rubbish such as sweet wrappers. The black cooking range would also provide heating and hot water, and this was often kept burning throughout the day and evening.

While Monday might be known as wash-day in many houses, Friday was a favourite (although perhaps not with the cook of the house) as this was baking day when bread, teacakes and sponge cakes were made for the weekend ahead.

For those wealthy enough to employ others, housework meant supervising the staff, deciding what tasks would be carried out on what day, and perhaps helping with menu decisions for the week ahead, and what groceries would be ordered in.

As for keeping yourself and the family clean, once again during this period some degree of manual labour was needed for working-class women. Until the 1950s or 1960s, many households didn't have an indoor bathroom, so a bath was a tin bath in front of the fire, which meant that hot water needed to be boiled up on the stove to fill it. Understandably, many families would have bath night only once a week, with one person after another using the same bathwater – ideally with the dirtiest person going in last.

There were also public baths where you could get washed and sometimes go for a swim under the same roof. These included Manningham Baths (opened in 1904), Windsor Baths and Five Lane Ends. Most of these facilities came into being between 1890 and 1910 and also incorporated washhouses. Saltaire was ahead of its time, with the Caroline Street bathhouse opening in 1863 and offering what was, for its time, an advanced washing facility where laundry could be washed, dried and ironed within a few hours. Titus Salt, founder of the model village Saltaire, reputedly disliked seeing washing hanging out to dry on washing lines. However, the Turkish and slipper baths seem not to have been popular with the villagers and they closed in 1894.

Shopping

For most, shopping was very much part of everyday life, particularly in an era when food shopping was done on a daily rather than a weekly basis, and mail order was the exception rather than the norm. Interestingly, Bradford did become home to at least three well-known catalogue firms, each of which was a major employer.

We would be surprised nowadays at the large variety of shops, with many created just for one purpose, such as a tobacconist, silversmith, coffee shop, watchmaker, tallow chandler, druggist, draper, printer, milliner, tailor, tea dealer, bookseller and spice merchant.

The shopping environment ranged from informal means of purchase, such as from street traders and door-to-door salespeople, through the likes of Kirkgate and Rawson Market, and on to the glamour of a department store such as Busby's, which was a real Bradford institution, with thousands of Bradfordians mourning its loss when it burnt down in 1979. Here, customers were often known by name, if they were regulars, and the store was known for treating customers and staff well. Staff were paid over the odds for shop work, while customers could enjoy courtesies such as chairs lined-up for people to sit on when in the sales queue, and a cup of tea brought along to those waiting to see the bargains.

Amy Busby (née Hibbard) was the wife of Ernest Busby, founder of the department store Busby's. She'd been a draper's apprentice before her marriage in 1895. The couple had four children – three boys, and a daughter named Rita, all of whom went on to be involved at the store.

It was Amy Busby who had the honour of carrying out the official opening of the store's new premises at its 'palace of merchandise' on Manningham Lane on 26 April 1930. The shop had the advantage of having a tram-stop right outside the store, so that people could travel in from the suburbs, including Manningham, Heaton and even Saltaire, step straight off the tram and through the doors into the warm shop, which was filled with goods of every kind.

And there really were goods aplenty – these new premises meant that Busby's could expand its stock by five times between 1931 and 1939. Furs were manufactured, cleaned and remodelled on site and women could also buy gloves, hats and trimmings, and have their dressmaking done at the store.

The store was much more than just a shop. For many families it was one of their annual or weekly treats – from the festive Father Christmas's grotto to meeting for a coffee on a Saturday. And for the harassed housewife, Busby's offered a place to unwind and socialise, with a library, café, hairdresser, beauty salon and record counter. Customer Doreen Baxter remembered:

Birthday treats and special occasions were often celebrated by a trip to Busby's. After a good look around, the highlight was tea in the café where Mr Busby always came to each table to talk to the children. I always loved the window display and in later years became a window dresser myself.

Those window displays became part of the shopping scene, with children craning their necks from passing buses and trams to see the Christmas display. No Bradford shop did Christmas quite like Busby's. On the day of their Christmas parade, thousands of people would line the route from central Bradford to the store, with children keeping a look-out for that first glimpse of Father Christmas coming along. Once inside, waiting boys and girls would be entertained by different things to look for while in the queue for Father Christmas, such as his fairy helper, waterfalls and moving models.

Another Bradford landmark was the Swan Arcade, which stood on the site of the former Old Swan Inn, opposite the Wool Exchange, and opened in 1880. This Italianate-style shopping mall was home to dozens of individual shops and tended to attract wealthier shoppers who wanted luxury and one-off goods for their homes. Among the many traders vying for the custom of those who strolled through the arcade in all their finery were E. Alexander & Son Wine, Spirit & Cigar Merchants, the Bradford Tailoring & Clothing Manufacturing Company, antique dealer and picture restorer Alfred Megson, and share broker George Battinson.

There was also a Lyon's Tea & Coffee Shop on Market Street, and Lingard's department store was well loved for serving what were said to be the best cup of tea and toasted teacakes in town, as well as for its overhead automatic change dispenser, which children particularly loved to watch.

Everyday street life

At the opposite end of the scale to the glamour of the department store and the beauty of the shopping arcade, goods peddled door-to-door or from a pitch on a street corner were often sold by those who couldn't find jobs elsewhere. Many sellers had nicknames related to what they sold, and these people were a familiar sight on the streets of Bradford, with some having a regular pitch where buyers could find them, and others walking the streets and alleyways getting customers where they could.

Judy Barrett's humbug shop

Judy Barrett was a sweet seller with a tiny shop in Westgate who became famous for her eponymously named humbugs. A newspaper story on the dismantling of the premises in 1879 reported that Judy had run the shop for 'three score years'. Judy, described as being 'homely in appearance', in her shop 'never noted for its palatial appearance' produced a humbug fulsomely described as 'large and luscious' and as much a part of a Saturday night in Bradford as the week's beef or mutton.

Judy had lived in the building adjoining the shop for her entire life and was also the custodian of the town's first public supply of water, which came from a reservoir behind the shop. She must have been a hard-working and resourceful soul since not only did she hold the key to the reservoir tap, charging people a half-penny for a bucket for water, and run the sweetshop, she was also a coal dealer often seen trudging from the pits at Low Moor carrying a sack of coal on her back accompanied by a donkey bearing the rest of the load.

Many of these people would otherwise have ended up in the workhouse if not for the work they did, and all of them would have faded from memory but for the work of artist John Sowden, an architect and property developer who painted portraits as a second career, operating from a studio in Stirling Street, close to Manchester Road. From here he painted more than 300 'street characters' between the years 1881 and 1906. He paid his subjects for their time – and must have had sympathetic qualities that allowed him to persuade the men, women and children he painted to abandon their job of work for a few hours and accompany him to his studio for a sitting.

Many of the portraits feature Bradford women, some born in the city and others who had arrived from elsewhere. Mary Ann Byrom lived in the deprived White Abbey area of town and was painted by Sowden in 1888, at the age of 63. She was known as 'Apple Mary' as she sold fruit and vegetables, firstly at Green Market and then, as old age and her increasing weight prevented travel, selling in the streets around Manningham.

Another character was 'Old Betty', who had been born in Grassington, real name Eliza Sunter. She sold ribbons, buttons and needles from a basket, wearing the white apron that seems to have been the favoured apparel of women hawkers. After her husband died, Old Betty shared her lodgings with a fellow female hawker, who she helped to care for from their lodgings in Bolton Road.

For many people, the cheap goods on sale from hawkers might have been their only meal of the day. Bridget Crown, captured in a typical hawking pose by Sowden, sold nettles around the alleyways of the Sun Inn – a cheap and nourishing plant that could be made into a nutritious broth.

Sowden attracted the disapproval of his Victorian colleagues for his street-life project. One day he came across a blind concertina-player named Ellen Hargreaves, who played outside the Midland Station, guided to her pitch by a child, probably in return for a few coppers. After the portrait sketches had been made at Sowden's studio, the artist and his subject found that the child guide had disappeared, no doubt exasperated by the wait. Sowden gallantly offered to help Ellen back to her pitch and, taking her arm to guide her, was subject to the disapproving stares of passing businessmen, astonished at seeing an artist and beggar walking along the street together.

Cockle Sarah

Perhaps the best known of Sowden's working-class subjects was Cockle Sarah, a colourful character who married a man named John Laycock in 1873, becoming involved in a bigamy scandal that was reported in the *Leeds Times*, and then subsequently widowed. Sarah sold cockles around the streets of Bowling and Bradford Moor, and became known to people of all classes, a fact attested to by the thousands of people who turned up to her wedding to William Garth in 1893 at Holy Trinity Church in Idle. Trams were brought to a standstill in Leeds Road as the guests crowded to the nuptials, and newspapers later reported: 'When the bridal party emerged from the church amid loud cheering, rice, peas, horse corn and other similarly indelicate confetti were showered on the happy pair.' Sarah was again widowed in later years and in 1909 moved in with her sister-in-law at Birkshall Lane in Bowling. Sadly, her life ended as a result of a fall down a flight of stairs, which broke her neck.

Markets were well-known for their lively and sometimes eccentric characters – both customers and traders. One of the best known was Kirkgate Market, which opened, on the site of an older market, in 1878. This was a great place to grab a bite to eat, perhaps from the pie & peas shop, or a piece of boiled fish or steak at the little penned-in areas where customers could plan which stalls to visit next while enjoying the hot food.

Rawson Market was known best for its fruit, vegetables and meat, and was generally the noisier of the two markets, with traders shouting out their wares and competing for customers, trying to be heard above the hubbub of shoppers.

CASE STUDIES

These two examples profile the home circumstances of two very different women – Catherine Salt, a wealthy woman who was married to the son of Titus Salt, and Margaret Sutton, a

Bradford woman from a background of poverty who was driven to commit a terrible crime that shocked the city.

Catherine Salt

Catherine and her husband Titus Salt Junior lived at Milner Field in Saltaire, a mansion created especially for the couple, which was honoured by royal visits during their time there. Catherine lived at the house until 1903, when she was forced to leave and sell the business after the death of her husband.

Sir Titus Salt himself had bought the land back in 1869 and Catherine and Titus Junior commissioned a new house that was built between 1871 and 1873 in the Neo Gothic style, with both the interior and the exterior of their home rich in style and glamour. The family enjoyed an opulent lifestyle with a telephone system to connect them to the mill, their own private water supply, a dairy, a kitchen garden with glasshouses, and a modern lighting system. Their mansion had ten bedrooms, dressing rooms, a butler's pantry and housekeeper's accommodation, as well as a billiard room and conservatory, the latter of which was lit with Chinese lanterns for one of the royal visits.

Catherine could take walks in the grounds, enjoying the hothouse plants in the conservatory, woodland walks and a stroll around the lake and fish pond. Salt Junior died just six months after welcoming Princess Beatrice and Prince Henry of Battenberg to Saltaire in 1887 and, by 1903, the Salt family's connection with Milner Field had ended. The house was demolished in the 1950s.

Margaret Sutton

The sad tale of Margaret Sutton, a Bradford woman who cut the throats of her two children and then tried to kill herself, dying in hospital a week later, made the headlines of newspapers across the UK in the winter of 1860.

At the time of the tragedy, Margaret was 34 years old and living on High Street (now Barkerend Road) in the Bowling area with 32-year-old John George Gowland, an attorney's clerk for Messrs Terry & Watson, and their two daughters, aged 4 and 2. Margaret seems to have been well-liked in the area, but behind closed doors was an unhappy woman, badly treated by her husband. Following the tragedy, the court case revealed that Margaret had written to friends and family saying she wanted to leave John Gowland but had been advised to stay for the sake of the children.

On the night of the killings Margaret was at home with the two girls in the squalid single room that served as their home. Driven to despair by her husband's behaviour and her terrible life, in a fit of mental anguish she took it upon herself to end the life of the children by cutting their throats and then tried to kill herself, being discovered by her husband when he returned later that night. Neighbours ran to the scene on hearing his cries and would eventually testify on Margaret's behalf, in a case which the *Bradford Observer* would call the tragedy of a 'poor unhappy frenzy-stricken mother'. Despite the severity of Margaret's crime, when her case was heard, public sympathy was with her for the way that Gowland had treated her in the run up to the murders.

After the death of her children, Margaret was taken to Bradford Infirmary where she was visited by the mayor and chief constable. The inquest found that Gowland had repeatedly promised he would marry Margaret but never followed through, and she finally suspected that he had been unfaithful, leading her to despair and to the terrible events which followed.

Margaret was buried with her children at Scholemoor Cemetery and crowds of more than 2,000 watched the funeral procession. Local people raised £25 for a gravestone by subscription, and the gravestone, which still stands in the cemetery, has an engraving of a woman with a child on each side of her.

Gowland was literally chased out of town after the hearing by a group of women who 'hustled him and used him rather roughly' when he'd been waiting to receive his wages as witness in the court case (he'd been very concerned about his expenses) and then when he tried to leave by train a few days later from the Midland Station, at around 10 p.m., a mob of men and boys harassed him. He continued his criminal career back in his north-east homeland where he appeared in local newspapers on other charges of embezzlement.

CHAPTER TWO

Education

❖

The history of education in Bradford is an interesting one, with the city boasting several impressive 'firsts', including some of the earliest nursery care in the country and the pioneering provision of school meals. Bradford was also one of the first places in the country to offer free education through the elementary school system.

As with so many opportunities for women throughout this book, the availability of education for females was to some extent determined by social status, wealth and location. Despite this, we'll discover strong-willed women who managed to either achieve great things, or enabled others to secure a good future, through the medium of education.

These women, particularly in the first half of the twentieth century, were fighting against a prevailing belief across all classes that education for girls and women was less important than that for boys and men, since it was felt that most women would go on to be wives and mothers and, therefore, not be active within the working world, or if they were, would be working in low-skilled jobs that required little education, perhaps dropping in and out of the work community as and when family circumstances fluctuated, or if extra money was needed.

The early years of education in Bradford

For the first twenty years, the only education available to any child in England was private – whether that was provided by a place of employment, within the home via a governess or private tutor, at a Sunday school or in a private school. Needless to say, the experience of being taught music and French by a governess in the drawing room of a beautifully-furnished home was a far different experience from being taught verses from the Bible in a draughty church hall after a hard week spent working in a mill.

The Education Act of 1870 allowed local governments to begin to provide primary education for those children not already within the system, and within a few years, schools started to be established. This Act had strong connections with Bradford, as it was drafted by William Edward Forster, Liberal MP for Bradford – and the man after whom Bradford Forster Square Railway Station is named.

The landmark Education Act, and the 1880 Education Act that followed it, made education compulsory between the ages of 5 and 10, and was succeeded by the 1902 Education Act, bringing in the provision of secondary education. By 1918, education was compulsory for children up to the age of 14, remaining so until the upper age limit changed to 15 in 1947. It would not be until 1973 that children were required to stay at school until age 16.

The first Bradford School Board of 1870 was an all-male affair, comprised largely of wealthy men from the upper echelons of society. These men were called upon to count the number of children in the town and then to work out what the deficit of school places was. The board discovered that around 2,000 school places were needed, which was a comparatively small number compared to other towns and cities of a similar size.

With the extent of the numbers determined, work was soon underway and, between April and August 1874, eight new school buildings were constructed – at Bowling Back Lane, Lilycroft, Whetley Lane, Barkerend, Lorne Street, Horton Bank Top, Ryan Street and Feversham Street. Between them, these would educate thousands of the city's children. These schools were set within working-class environments dominated by the textile trade.

Children playing in the streets would have watched as workmen toiled on the buildings, knowing that soon their games would be halted by the need to go to school. And those who had attended private lessons sporadically, or who had been young workers earning money for the family, would soon enter the world of school and be bound, for better or worse, by the rules. Many of these children lived in conditions of poverty, were poorly nourished and badly clothed. But someone was about to turn up who would change the face of education in the UK forever. Her name was Margaret McMillan and her arrival in town can be called, with no exaggeration, a landmark moment in the city's history.

Margaret McMillan

Born in Westchester County, New York, in 1860, Margaret came to Bradford in 1892 with her sister Rachel. Westchester, a bustling state in New York county, had a railroad system that had caused a population boom as immigrants entered the region. At the time of Margaret's birth, the county was home to some 99,000 people – the McMillans were some of just a few leaving the county at a time when thousands were coming in from the opposite direction to find work.

In her autobiography *Life of Rachel McMillan*, Rachel memorably described the winter evening that the sisters reached Bradford:

> We arrived on a stormy night in November. Coming out from the entrance of the Midland station, we saw, in a swuther of rain, the shining statue of Richard Oastler standing in the Market Square, with two black and bowed little mill-workers standing at his knee.
>
> Next morning we awoke in a new and quite unknown world. It was a Sunday, and the smoke cloud that usually enveloped the city had lifted. Tall dark chimneys reaching skywards like monstrous trees, made dark outlines against the faint grey of the sunny morning. On

weekdays these big stone monsters belched forth smoke as black as pitch that fell in choking clouds.

> The condition of the poorer children was worse than anything that was described or painted. It was a thing that this generation is glad to forget. The neglect of infants, the utter neglect almost of toddlers and older children, the blight of early labour, all combined to make of a once vigorous people a race of undergrown and spoiled adolescents; and just as people looked on at the torture two hundred years ago and less, without any great indignation, so in the 1890s people saw the misery of poor children without perturbation.

Strong words – and the Macmillan sisters would prove that they were women of action. During their time in London, the pair had founded the Open-Air Nursery School & Training Centre and it was this enlightened thinking that worked in the slums of Deptford that would now benefit poorer children in Bradford. The problems of the Deptford Docklands were not a million miles away from those of Victorian Bradford. Both areas had a large population of children with parents living at subsistence level, people with precious little time or money to invest in making sure that their children had an education. Every day was a struggle just to keep the family fed and clothed.

Right from the beginning of her time in Bradford, Margaret was involved in politics as a member of the Independent Labour Party and came to the city just a year after the end of the bitter Lister Mills strike (see Chapter 7).

In 1894, Margaret was elected as the Independent Labour Party's candidate for the Bradford School Board, and this appointment gave her an influence on what happened in the borough's schools, after twenty years of dominance from a largely male school board. Along with the city's medical officer Dr James Kerr, Margaret undertook the first medical inspection of young schoolchildren. The findings of their report, which showed a desperate need for nutrition and cleanliness among the city's young population, prompted a call for schools to install bathrooms for the children and to provide a badly needed free school meal for each child.

Many children lived in poverty. Margaret's theory was that a child couldn't be expected to work well at school if he or she was hungry, tired or wearing inadequate clothing. With an enlightened attitude way ahead of her time, she realised that not all home-based problems, such as lack of money or poor housing, could be solved easily at root and instead she focused on trying to make sure that at least the school, if not the home, could provide a nurturing environment not only for the child's educational needs, but also with a focus on their nutrition, warmth and cleanliness.

For a young child living in a back-to-back terrace with a shared privy and washing facilities, and perhaps just a small fire burning in the grate even in the depths of winter, the facilities on offer at school must have seemed almost unbelievable and perhaps it would have even been quite overwhelming to walk into an airy, heated building to find that food and milk were available, along with bathrooms and hand-washing facilities, and there was even somewhere warm and comfortable to lie down for an afternoon nap.

Bradford was one of the UK's pilot cities selected to try out the fledgling school meals system. Between April and July 1907, a group of 'necessitous children' was given a course of meals consisting of breakfast and lunch. The children were selected because of their home circumstances. Some came from large families with little food to go round, others had a breadwinner out of work.

The experiment makes for poignant reading. Efforts were made to make mealtimes as pleasant as possible, with staff going as far as having the dining table laid with tablecloths and flowers, and even junior waitresses on hand to serve the food. However, it was remarked afterwards that the tablecloths became soiled because of the filthy state of the clothing of some of the children, while several youngsters were so dirty they were unable to get their hands and faces properly clean before the meal began. Breakfast was porridge with milk and treacle, followed by bread and dripping, with milk to drink – solid if unremarkable fare.

Over the years Margaret wrote several books which, in time, influenced thinking on child health and education, including the 1896 *Child Labour and the Half Time System and Early Childhood*. Her work came to fruition in 1906 with the passing of the Provision of School Meals Act, allowing all schoolchildren the right to a midday meal. Her name lives on at Margaret McMillan Tower on Princes Way, currently home to the central library.

Miriam Lord

Born in Bradford in 1885, just seven years before Margaret McMillan arrived in the city, Miriam Lord was the woman who would put McMillan's Open-Air Schooling theories into practise.

Miriam progressed from working as a baker to becoming an unqualified teacher at Belle Vue Secondary School, gaining a teaching qualification in 1908 at Saffron Waldren and eventually working her way up to superintendent of Lilycroft Open-Air Nursery School in 1921. Open-air schooling is almost unknown nowadays, but in the 1920s it was at the cutting edge of educational thinking. Bradford had one of the country's first open-air schools, which attracted educationalists from around the UK who were keen to see this type of teaching in action.

Miriam launched an appeal to build a memorial to her former colleague, raising £20,000 towards the Margaret McMillan College, which opened in 1952.

Miriam's work was recognised when she was awarded an Order of the British Empire (OBE) for services to nursery and community education and she is remembered on a blue heritage plaque, and in the name of the Manningham school, Miriam Lord Primary, which stands in the former textile community close to where much of her pioneering work was carried out.

The Open-Air School movement

Bradford in the 1920s, with its polluted post-First World War landscape, may not have seemed the first choice for an open-air schooling system, but this city was the place where Miriam Lord set up open-air schools, at Lilycroft Road and Princeville, both industrial, working-class areas which, like many areas of the city, were characterised by narrow streets of terraced housing, blighted by air pollution and industrial waste. Other schools followed at Thackley (Buck Wood), Odsal and Heaton.

Thackley Open-Air School opened in 1908 and its pupil-patients were boys and girls who weren't robust enough to thrive at a normal school – they might have had diarrhoea from slum toilets or chest problems because of constant exposure to air pollution. Forty 'delicate' children were brought in by tram for the first intake. The classrooms had the same facilities as many of their inner-city counterparts, the difference being that one side of the building was open to the elements, since exposure to the outdoors was believed to be beneficial to those with health problems.

The open-air system was also in vogue within the medical system at this time – both tuberculosis and polio patients were also treated in open-air wards around the UK, with one patient being a young Mary Berry, who went on to become the famous home baker.

SECONDARY EDUCATION

After the Education Act of 1902, higher grade schools and secondary schools were recognised by the Board of Education and schooling was opened to a wider age group than ever before, keeping teenagers out of the workplace and putting them into further education. The free-place system granted by act of parliament gave a £5 grant to schools for each pupil aged 12 to 18, provided that the school was open to all children in the surrounding area.

However, although it was now official policy that every child was entitled to a secondary education, this was easier said than done. In a city such as Bradford, where the opportunities for young teenagers to earn money could be plentiful, for example in the textile industry, many families expected and needed children to start earning as soon as possible in order to contribute to the family budget. Also, in communities where few had been educated beyond the age of 12, there could be a social expectation that things continued as they were and that education was only for the wealthy. And, of course, it would take a strong-minded teenager to ask her family whether she could continue her schooling while she watched other local girls take jobs and enjoy the pocket money and social life that went with them.

By 1908, there were thirteen public secondary schools in the Bradford district – six for girls, six for boys and one for both. As well as organising education for pupils, school boards also had to organise the training of teachers via an apprentice scheme. This scheme was one way a bright girl could progress beyond the official school leaving age and go into a steady career. At the starting age of 14, the pupil teacher could earn £10 a year, increasing by £2-10s per year for five years. Pupil teachers taught for half-time and were themselves taught to be teachers for the remainder of the time. For a girl from a non-affluent background who was ambitious and had parents who were prepared to accept the lower wages of the scheme when compared to working, for example, in a textile mill, this was a way to eventually move into a respected and middle-class profession with comparative ease.

Bradford Girls' Grammar School

Perhaps the city's best-known school for girls is Bradford Girls' Grammar School, founded in 1875, more than a quarter of a century before the 1902 Education Act made secondary education widely available, and offering girls in the town their first chance to benefit from a secondary education.

The sum of £5,000 for the school building was raised by a group of citizens, including a Mrs Byles, members of the Ladies' Educational Association and the aforementioned MP W.E. Forster.

The school was opened by Lady Frederick Cavendish on 28 September 1875, in the premises of a former private school on Hallfield Road, close to White Abbey Road. Excitement was at a high as those who had helped to raise funds gathered at the opening ceremony to see the building their money had helped to purchase, although a further £2,000 was still required to make the site fit for purpose. 'A new educational era for girls has begun', was the stirring message the audience was given at the opening ceremony.

Headmistress Miss Porter informed her audience that she hoped that what she taught the first pupils of this new school would stay with them throughout their lives and they would learn a few subjects at a time thoroughly, rather than trying to cram in too many subjects at once. She also warned that parents must avoid retarding the advancement of their children by taking them out for a half-day holiday here and there.

The school's fee was 4 guineas a term, with some scholarships available for children whose parents couldn't afford the fee, as the school was initially made up of pupils from the surrounding Manningham district – the children of merchants and textile barons, for example.

The school flourished in the years before the First World War, with 'old girls' mentioned on the school Honours Board as going on to careers as lawyers and headmistresses after attending universities including Oxford and Cambridge. Barbara Betts (who became Barbara Castle) is one of the school's most famous old girls (see Chapter 4).

Elizabeth Denby, born in 1894, was also a Bradford Girls' Grammar School pupil and went on to study at the London School of Economics. She became a social housing expert, helping to create wartime furniture, and organised the Living in Houses exhibition in London.

At the coming of war, Bradford Girls' Grammar played its part in the war effort by taking in Belgian refugees, and knitting socks for soldiers on the Front; like so many other community groups across the city.

The year 1925 saw the school's jubilee celebrations and, in 1936, new premises at Lady Royd, close to the present-day Bradford Royal Infirmary, were opened by Mary, Princess Royal. The new accommodation included a gymnasium, an arts hall and science labs.

In the Second World War the girls were evacuated to Settle, with the Lady Royd buildings bizarrely then providing a rest centre for women and children who had, in turn, been evacuated from the south of England.

Belle Vue Girls' School

Two years after the foundation of Bradford Girls' Grammar School, Belle Vue Girls' School was founded as the Girls' Higher Grade School. It began in premises on Manningham Lane, at the heart of a prosperous middle-/upper-class district and, in 1904, became Belle Vue Girls' Secondary School. Attendance cost 2½ pennies per week and the first headteacher was Emily Holmes. The only other staff were two assistant teachers and a pupil teacher.

Within a year the school had outgrown its premises and moved to a new building in Heaton, which had cost over £15,000. These new premises meant for the first time that pupils could go from infant through to secondary school on one site.

In 1884, Sarah Louise Beszant became headmistress and would hold the post for forty years. During her tenure, there would be many changes in attitudes towards schooling for girls and she had many progressive ideas, for instance she introduced chemistry and physiology to the curriculum in an era when these were not seen as suitable subjects for girls. She also encouraged her pupils to take part in sports. During her years of leadership, the school became a Higher Grade School and then a Secondary School.

ADULT EDUCATION FOR WOMEN

As well as pioneering nursery school education and the care of young children within the education system, Bradford also provided education at the other end of the age spectrum, with vocational and non-vocational education for adults.

Leaving school at the age of between 12 and 14 was very much the norm for girls of all classes. Some wealthy girls might be lucky enough to go to college or university, but for others, becoming part of the wage-earning population at the official working age was a must for family finances. Many women must have longed to carry on at school, however, even after starting work, options were available to continue education for those with the means and self-discipline to carry on – either through on the job training or with evening classes that taught either a hobby or a skill related to a job or career.

As with school education, the education of women lagged behind that of men. In 1825, the Mechanics' Institute was founded to help educate the working men of the town. However, it would be another twenty-five years before women were able to attend its classes. This establishment was the fore-runner of Bradford Technical School, which went on to become the University of Bradford in the 1960s. It is worth mentioning that the University of Bradford received its Royal Charter in 1966, becoming the fortieth university to open in Britain, and offering people from the city and beyond the chance to receive a degree-level education within the city.

Women from moneyed families were freer to pursue their hobbies and interests during their leisure time, particularly if these were traditional pursuits, such as needlework, painting or writing. For working women, things were more difficult, and this is where evening classes came in. In 1857, the Bradford Female Educational Institute opened, offering a library and evening classes.

A crowd of 170 women attended the opening night, with classes running from 7 p.m. to 9 p.m. – no mean feat for an adult pupil who had worked a full day in a labour-intensive role. Anyone attending these classes after a hard day at work – having to rush through the household chores and prepare an evening meal, before travelling to the institute – had real determination, and this must have made for a positive atmosphere as these women would have placed real value on the knowledge they were gaining.

To begin with, the institute concentrated on equipping its female pupils with the basics of reading and writing, since many were barely literate, having left school at a young age to bring money in for the family.

Despite the excitement of the early years, not everyone approved of the education of women and in 1859, the lord mayor stepped in to advise members of the institute to ignore critical voices by those like a man who wrote to the *Bradford Observer* to ask who would marry the women who'd educated themselves to be above the 'drudgery and toil' needed to keep a poor man's house and children.

Education in Saltaire

The women of Saltaire had opportunities for adult education too. Because the village of Saltaire was a purpose-built settlement, from the time it was complete, buildings had been created with the purpose of leisure and education in mind. Both the Saltaire Institute and the schools were far ahead of what was on offer elsewhere within the county during our period.

The institute, now known as the Victoria Hall, was completed in 1871 at a cost of £25,000. With its 200-seat lecture hall, gymnasium, reading room and library of 8,500 books, it offered a central place for educationally-minded villagers to gather.

The institute also acted as a meeting place for village groups, such as Northcliff Women Golfers and the Shipley Women's Unionists Association.

Fanny Hertz

Fanny Hertz (1830-1908) was the daughter of a diamond merchant who, along with her yarn merchant husband William David Hertz, filled her home at Ashfield Place in Little Horton with writers, intellectuals and radicals, who regularly met for socialising.

Fanny believed in education for women, noting 'the social position of women everywhere and always corresponds exactly with a degree of civilisation of the community at large'. The neglect of female education, she believed, would lead to:

> neglected and unhealthy children; the slatternly appearance, and rude, uncouth manners of the young working men and women; cheerless comfortless homes, badly-cooked meals, ill-mannered expenditure; in extravagant, unsuitable dress, in frowning looks, angry words and family jarrings …

In 1857 she helped set up the Women's Educational Institute at Horton Road in Bradford, which at its height had 600 students enrolled. However, within a few short years, it was run by a male-dominated group. Students learnt the three Rs, as well as making their choice from classes that included needlework, history, natural science and geography.

CHAPTER THREE

Votes for Women and the Suffrage Campaign

❖

The votes for women campaign was not a single united stand but a multi-faceted cause with many different aspects, personalities and means of approach, ranging from the 'tread softly' tactic of allowing men to gain the vote before attempting to get it for women, through to the hard-line method of burning buildings and smashing windows to gain attention for votes for women.

Votes for women captivated people everywhere, no matter what their stance – whether people were talking about the suffragettes with their militant actions on hunger strikes and in prison, or the suffragists who overcame their fears and reticence to speak up in public and took their suffrage caravan around Yorkshire – in their own way as brave as the headline-grabbing suffragettes. Many women had seen their Victorian mothers grow up with basic reading and writing skills and no job prospects, and in this new Edwardian era they wanted more for themselves. Since 1870, education had been more widely available and children were learning more than their parents had and realising that there were opportunities out there they were missing out on.

Although there had been a female chartist association in Bradford since 1841, which campaigned for the male working-class vote, the first demand for women's votes received by Parliament came from a group of Yorkshire females in 1882, led by Pudsey woman Elizabeth Wolstenholme Elmy, who lived just a few miles away. The antics of the London suffragettes may have pulled in most of the attention and headlines, but the city had many remarkable women who stepped forward to support the cause and, whether campaigning in public in Bradford or outside the Houses of Parliament, the women had plenty to contribute, with memorable and attention-grabbing methods of campaigning.

Background

Although many think of votes for women within an Edwardian context with women marching on Parliament, spurred on by campaigners such as Emmeline Pankhurst, the cause actually had its roots in the Chartism campaign of the Victorian era, which aimed to gain political rights for working men. Millions of people signed the demands for six rights for working-class males and it was this movement that paved the way for women decades later.

The six rights

These are a vote for all men over 21, the secret ballot, no property qualification to become a M.P., payment for M.P.s, equally-sized electoral districts, annual parliamentary elections.

Many working-class men got the vote in the reforms of 1867 and 1884, and by the turn of the century could vote to send their own politicians to parliament. Now, radical suffragists wanted the vote for women so they could improve working conditions, and a way to do this was to become involved in politics.

By 1900, around seventy per cent of men owned or rented property and were entitled to vote – at last some working-class men had rights. Encouraged by this, women began to stand for local government. Yet their success begged the question of why could they stand on committees such as that of a board of guardians or a school board but not be allowed to be full members of British society with their own vote?

During this last full year of the reign of Queen Victoria, word crossed the Pennines that Lancashire women, many from the textile trade, were meeting during summer evenings in outdoor gatherings, working with the growing Labour movement to change conditions and be able to vote to join in with politics. Although the Liberal party had promised to work for the cause if they got into power, many women were frustrated that their wages were so much lower than their male counterparts. Their frustration was echoed from the 1890s when *The Clarion* newspaper, widely read in working-class communities, discussed the pros and cons of the issue and the rights of working women.

For mass appeal, the new Independent Labour Party, formed in Bradford against a background of industrial strife, had more sympathy with the women than other political parties. Its branches welcomed women members and let them take an active part in party life, along with organisations such as the Women's Co-operative Guild.

Suffragist or suffragette?

The National Union of Women's Suffrage Societies (NUWSS), founded in 1897, aimed to gain women's suffrage through 'peaceful and legal means'. Its members tended to avoid violent or fierce protests, such as smashing windows and blowing up pillar boxes, and many felt that the behaviour of more militant suffragettes put those wanting votes for women in a bad light.

When the First World War broke out, the NUWSS supported the war effort and helped to staff hospital wards and create an employment agency for people to fill empty vacancies. By the outbreak of war in 1914, there were NUWSS branches in Heaton, Horton, Girlington, East Ward and Shipley.

The NUWSS stance was very much at odds with that of the Women's Social and Political Union (WSPU), founded in 1903 by Emmeline Pankhurst. WSPU's campaigning took place between 1903 and 1917 and their hard-hitting protests made them tough to ignore. No matter what people's political stance, high profile acts such as hunger strikes, burning empty buildings and smashing windows made the union unpopular with some men and women, with even many of those who supported votes for women feeling that WSPU was doing more harm than good.

The slogan of WSPU was 'deeds not words' and the group was for women only. From 1907, they were organised enough to hold women's parliaments, and their distinctive purple, white and green colours could be seen on banners, badges and so on. The Bradford branch was formed in 1906 and among its members were a Mrs Armitage of Little Horton, who acted as the first secretary, and Julia Varley, a mill-worker who became secretary of the Bradford Weavers and Textile Workers' Union and went on to play a leading role in the votes for women campaign in the pre-First World War years.

Before 1908, WSPU was able to draw attention to its cause via chalked advertisements for its meetings on pavements around the city, where they were a colourful call to action. However, in 1908, this practice was banned in the city, so members resorted to using chalkboards set up in the streets with sketched caricatures. This chalking issue was one that councils up and down the country had to contend with, and not just for suffragettes as businesses attempted to advertise their wares and other groups advertised their meetings.

The term 'suffragette' was first coined in January 1906 by the *Daily Mail* who, within two months, had the Pankhursts on their front pages. Yet, despite these new headline-grabbing protests, tens of thousands of women around the UK had been in suffrage societies for years. We know less about the non-militants simply because their actions weren't recorded in the newspapers. Unlike suffragettes, suffragists didn't actively court publicity with hard-hitting protests. Traditional suffragist societies asked only for women to have a property-based vote, whereas for radical societies this was demanded for all women over 21.

Votes for women – the local picture

Votes for women had its roots in the male suffrage campaign of the early Victorian era. In the 1840s, Bradford became part of agitation for male suffrage, with more than 5,000 men and women attending a rally for this at Temperance Hall in 1848. Then, on a hot day in August 1864, Lord Palmerston turned up to lay the foundation stone for the Wool Exchange in Market Street and was greeted by absolute silence rather than the cheers and applause of the crowd. He was seen as the barrier to working men getting the vote and, as such, was subjected to an intimidating vote of silence.

A few years later, the town's women gained a supporter in Liberal MP Edward Miall who, in 1869, promised:

> Happy will be the day when in England and throughout the world… woman takes her real and proper position – as companion and men's helpmeet in national affairs … We shall have gentler politics when the gentle sex takes to politics.

By the 1880s, the protest had grown to include votes for women as well as men and the *Leeds Times* reported in the winter of 1881 of a demonstration that it estimated had involved 3,000 protesters. Women from all around the country were part of the protest, and telegrams of support were read out to the crowd from groups around the UK who wished to be there in spirit. Active participants on the day included local women whose names would crop up more than once for the cause. They included Miss Glyde (Saltaire), Mrs Brooke of Wyke and Mrs McLaren of Bradford. The overriding argument of the night was that if W.E. Forster had allowed women to sit on school boards, why then could they not have the vote?

Bradford-based campaigns

The suffragists and suffragettes may have had different aims when it came to gaining the vote, but there was certainly no shortage of ideas, energy and initiative in the city when the campaign was running. Between 1907 and the end of the First World War, there were several high-profile campaigns.

In May 1907, there had been a mass meeting at the Mechanics' Institute where more than 250 people paid to come into the meeting of the WSPU. Chairman Mr R. Lishman acknowledged there had been complaints about the violence of the campaign, but stated that this was the only way to overturn laws. After all, the House of Commons had only gained its power by beheading one king and sending another into exile, he argued.

Campaign stalwart Julia Varley set forward a motion that women should gain the vote on the same terms as men, while a Mrs Martel stood up to announce that she'd seen women in Australia gain the vote when she lived there and maybe the women of Bradford should copy their sisters in Finland and refuse to do household chores until they got the vote – then they'd have it within twenty-four hours, she said, to laughter. However, she was interrupted during her speech and the chairman had to thank her for her contribution and deplore the friction at the meeting, where some believed that total male suffrage should be fought for first and tried to shout down anyone who took a more hard-line view.

And it wasn't just in suffrage meetings that women were shouted down. Some women suffered public condemnation because of their beliefs. Also in 1907, a Mrs Fielding of Bradford, who had been imprisoned for the cause, reported that one of her suffrage comrades had received a letter from an MP who warned her she was doing no good for votes for women and, although the WSPU had been excellent and stirred up public interest, these latest actions meant the battle would probably be lost. This woman had also watched one of her children lose her job because of the mother's involvement in the campaign, which had seen her sent to prison.

Mass protest at Shipley Glen

Adela Pankhurst, the youngest of the Pankhurst sisters, who hailed from Manchester, toured the north of England during the votes for women campaign, drumming up support through her rousing speeches, including one in Bradford. She was regional organiser for WSPU's West Yorkshire branch and organised public meetings that drew large crowds.

One of her most successful meetings was a 1908 mass public rally at Shipley Glen, a popular beauty spot a couple of miles from Bradford. The Glen was a well-loved stretch of moorland, trees and a brook that could attract thousands of day-trippers, who travelled up on the tram through the woods to emerge onto the Glen, with its far-reaching views of church steeples, chimneys, city streets and open countryside beyond.

However, nothing like this had been seen on Shipley Glen before. Between 40,000 and 100,000 participants (estimates vary) attended what Emmeline called a 'triumph for our cause' in the *Votes for Women* paper of June 1908.

In the next issue of the paper she gave more details, writing:

> For weeks past all Bradford has been talking about the Yorkshire Suffrage Sunday held in Shipley Glen on May 31st. The Tramway Committee made special preparations to convey the extra passengers expected, and for some days official notices appeared in all cars announcing the demonstration. The meeting was advertised to begin at 3.30 p.m., but before noon heavily laden cars began to leave the city, and an unending stream of people on foot wended their way to the picturesque glen, the property of the people of Bradford, about three miles away from the city itself.
>
> When the speakers arrived on the ground, the six platforms were surrounded by dense crowds numbering at least 100,000 people. Never in the history of the glen have so many human beings been gathered together. In the local Liberal Press there had appeared paragraphs suggesting that attempts would be made to disturb the meetings and this suggestion was seized upon by small gangs of noisy youths armed with bells and tin trumpets and so on.

> Nevertheless, the vast audience of orderly and attentive persons prevented any effective disturbance, and at 5 o' clock a resolution calling upon the Government to enfranchise the women of this country this session was carried with practical unanimity.
>
> When the meeting closed the people would not go away and begged us to hold another meeting in the evening. The Prime Minister expects us to show a popular demand for votes for women. We offer to him the demand of the people of Bradford, which has already spoken officially through its City Council when it adopted some months ago, a resolution similar to the one carried at the great open-air meeting on the Suffrage Sunday of Yorkshire.

Two years later, Emmeline's older sister Adela was one of those who helped disrupt MP Winston Churchill's visit to Bradford to raise publicity for the cause. The *Telegraph & Argus* reported on two women hiding in St George's Hall the night before:

> The following day found them thirsty, dishevelled and unwashed, but with hearts on fire for their cause.

A small number of Bradford women took part in the 'no vote, no census' UK-wide protest of 1911, whereby women deliberately occupied a house on census night in order to provide a marked protest when the census enumerator called round to record their details. However, in Bradford this proved something of a damp squib when only a small number of women occupied a house on Manningham Lane and refused to provide details of who was in the dwelling, writing only 'no vote, no census', rather than the name, age and birthplace of the occupants of the household. One house and a few women seemed just a token rather than a city-wide protest.

The year 1913 saw two of the most high-profile Bradford protests. First was the dyeing of the reservoir at Chellow Dene, which was turned a rich shade of purple overnight after being discoloured by textile dye. This was believed to be the work of suffragettes because, although no literature or symbols of the cause were left behind (as was sometimes the case after such acts when clues seemed to be left deliberately), a handbag was found containing traces of dyestuffs used in Bradford mills. This, and the size of the paper bags found nearby, led police to conclude that at least 14lb of dye, a large amount that would have had to be carried by at least two people, had been brought to the site to colour the water. However, the perpetrators had left little to incriminate themselves and the case had to be dropped.

Later that year was the Shirley Manor fire in which a historic mansion was burnt down. 'A Yorkshire mansion destroyed – women's further folly' thundered the *Yorkshire Evening Post*. The mansion had been built for Mr John Taylor of Birstall, and was portrayed in Charlotte Brontë's *Shirley*. Around £5,000-worth of damage was done to the empty mansion, which was undergoing renovation. The fire was discovered at around 3am by a passing police constable and reports indicated that several different fires had been started around the house, leading to the destruction of around thirty rooms. Five postcards were found at the site, one of which read:

> Votes for women. Forcible feeding failed. The Cat and Mouse Act also failed. Forcible feeding will also fail again. You can't keep rebels in prison.

That year, several other fires around the city led people to believe that suffragettes were behind this, following a spate of high-profile blazes across the country, often targeting abandoned buildings or large mansions. Between April and June, there were more than thirty major fires including at Barkerend Mill and Drummond's Mill.

The wider UK picture

Of course, the Bradford votes for women supporters weren't acting independently but were part of a national demonstration, which saw meetings, protests and rallies in towns and cities up and down the country. Just as women such as Adela Pankhurst came to Bradford as part of a speaking tour, so too did the women of Bradford travel to other towns and cities to show their support at votes for women events. For example, Leeds was just a train ride away and here, women such as Leonara Cohen inspired hundreds of others to join the cause through rousing speeches and gatherings.

In February 1908, a number of Bradford women were involved in a raid on Parliament organised by the National, Social and Political Union. It was a two-pronged attack where twenty-one women tried to leap out of a van in Old Palace Yard, while others tried to storm the House of Commons. Fifty people were arrested and a 'good deal of disorder' occurred.

Newspapers recorded the names, ages and occupations of those involved and among the Bradford women were Annie W. Bachelor aged 42 of Idle (married), Louisa Laycock, a weaver aged 35 and Lizzie Glyde, age 38 and married. Those involved ranged from their early 20s to their early 60s. What a newspaper called 'ladies of refinement and education' were taken to court in Westminster for insulting behaviour and obstruction, where one Superintendent Wells reported that more than 200 police had been involved in stopping the women storming the gates at Old Palace Yard with their shouts of 'Votes for women!'. They were given sureties of £20 for twelve months, or six weeks in prison.

Households up and down the country would have discussed the case over breakfast or their evening meal, as newspapers from across the UK reported on the case and its aftermath. The women told a spokesperson they were 'well and cheerful' and saw their heavy sentences as an indication that the government was afraid of their agitation. The *Leeds Mercury* ran a special report: *The Yorkshire Suffragettes – who's who among those arrested*. 'All the expenses of women making the journey to London are paid for by the central authority', it was stated.

For another rally that same year, a notice was placed in the *Bradford Telegraph* stating that a special train was travelling from Bradford to take anyone who'd like to go to London and support the women. It announced proudly that the Bradford

Social and Political Women's Union would be bringing along a large banner that had cost more than £14 and proclaimed: 'We demand the right to vote and the power to serve. Grant to womanhood the justice England should be proud to give.'

Women came from as far as Aberdeen for this event, which was again extensively covered in papers the country over and eagerly discussed in homes, streets and workplaces across the land. But despite the excitement that often seemed to accompany such rallies, enthusiasm could be patchy. A year before, a meeting in Bradford addressed by none other than Adela Pankhurst attracted only a 'sparse attendance' (including just one male) at the Friends' Meeting House on Manningham Lane. 'Votes for women has not sufficient magnetic influence in Bradford to draw the average woman through showers of rain to a meeting on the subject,' a reporter wrote acidly, even suggesting that the solitary male was just in the room to escape the weather.

Votes for women – individuals

The suffragette movement might have had a lot of its focus in and around London, particularly the Houses of Parliament, however, the northern towns certainly had a passion for the cause and contributed several prominent suffragettes, including Adela Pankhurst, Edith Key and Lilian Armitage.

Perhaps the most prominent Bradford suffragette was Julia Varley OBE, who was known around the UK for her commitment to the cause. Here was a lady determined to root out what she saw as social injustices. She was a member of the Bradford Board of Guardians for three years and, to gain experience of the life of tramps and gain the confidence of homeless people, she disguised herself as a tramp and toured round Yorkshire and Lancashire, 'making special investigations in the tramp wards' of workhouses, then writing a series of articles.

Lilian Armitage who, during her suffragette years, lived at 81 Tivoli Place in Horton, was a formidable addition to the city's votes for women campaign. She acted as secretary for the

Bradford branch of the WSPU and, when fellow protesters were imprisoned for their activities, helped carry out the 'household duties' to keep life running smoothly at home.

Edith Key was another prominent activist, born in 1872 in Eccleshill to an 18-year-old millworker mother named Grace Proctor. No father was named on her birth certificate. However, her father may have been a local mill owner of means as, when Edith was 10 weeks old, her mother and Joseph Fawcett signed a lawyer's agreement for Joseph to pay Grace a £25 down payment and 2s per week until Edith was 13. By her mid-20s, Grace was working at the Britannia Inn with the pub landlord (a widow) and his children, while her own children were cared for by Edith's aunts. As a teenager, Edith moved to Huddersfield and worked as a half-timer and, by the age of 18, was a knotter and a member of Huddersfield Choral Society. She married a blind musician who worked as a piano tutor. Edith had two children and eventually became secretary of the WSPU. She also sheltered suffragettes when the Cat and Mouse Act was at its height.

Isabella Ford had been inspired by what she saw as the hypocrisy of her Liberal employers after the great Manningham strike, and she joined the Independent Labour Party, which championed women textile workers of the country. She helped set up the NUWSS.

Mrs Henry Muff – wife of Mr Henry Muff, of drapery firm Brown, Muff & Co – was a very active leader of women's political movements in Bradford for many years.

In October 1893, Gertrude Helen Taylor Glyde is mentioned as the third daughter of the late W.E. Glyde of Moorhead, Saltaire, director of Salts Mill. *The Shipley Times* of 19 March 1908 reported that a Mrs C.A. Glyde had been released after being sentenced in London for disorder. Her husband came to Holloway to fetch her home.

Margaret Holden Illingworth (1842-1919) was, in 1913, president of the Bradford Women's Suffrage Society and vice-president of the London Society for Women's Suffrage and the NUWSS, despite her husband Alfred not being a supporter. She had six sons and may have had to fight the cause at home as well as in everyday life.

The anti-suffrage movement

Not all women wanted the vote at the start of the suffrage campaign of the Victorian age. For older women, it had been within their lifetime that only the elite had the vote (until the Reform Act of 1867) and, after seeing some working men enfranchised in 1884, to see women gain the vote too may have seemed like a lot of change too soon. And while others may have agreed with the sentiment, they often didn't like the methods – different organisations had different ways of approaching the cause.

Opposition to suffrage could be strong, even as late as 1917, as a man named W.M. Cheshire wrote to his local newspaper. He said that the vote shouldn't be given to women with five million men away fighting:

> There is something incongruous about the notion that by giving certain women the right to vote at a parliamentary election the solution of complex political problems will be facilitated. The vast majority are women whose aptitudes, ambitions and maternal duties make them shrink from responsibilities and duties of a public and political nature … in the larger Imperial questions of finance, foreign affairs, defence, trade, and transport, woman's temperament and inexperience would make her a hindrance instead of a help.

Regularly, women came up against opposition from men and even other women, and some of the compliments were veiled, such as when Mr W. Claridge, in 1905, a prospective Liberal candidate for the Western Division of Bradford, told the Shipley Liberal Club he couldn't understand why women could vote for town councils, boards of guardians, and yet not be able to give a parliamentary vote. However, he did understand 'a man objecting to women serving on any public body'. He also added: 'the vote of the women would tend to raise the tone of political life.'

Of course, the women of Bradford and elsewhere faced vehement opposition to their cause, sometimes from their own families, neighbours, workmates and even other members of the cause who may have belonged to a different sector of the campaign.

Whole societies were dedicated to opposing and mocking those who demanded votes for women, with some sectors attempting to make campaigners look ridiculous, anti-patriotic and unfeminine. The Women's National Anti-Suffrage League, founded on 21 July 1908 in Bradford, had both male and female members and merged with a national male organisation in 1910 to form the National League for Opposing Woman Suffrage.

Votes for women at last

The tragedy of the Great War brought the votes for women campaign to its conclusion sooner than otherwise would have happened. The government was unable to ignore the issue of votes for women after seeing females in action, doing jobs traditionally reserved for men, throughout the war years. Women had literally kept the home fires burning, turning their hand to everything from tram driving to munitions work – often working in as much danger as some of their male counterparts in the armed forces.

Not everyone agreed with the way women fought for the cause, but by 1919, it was obvious that it would only be a matter of time before all adult females had the vote – something that was achieved in 1928, a decade after the end of the Great War.

CHAPTER FOUR

Campaigning and Politics

❖

When it came to politics and public affairs, women had a wide range of options during this period, from the sociability of the Co-operative Women's Guild and the Women's Institute to the many different political groups that have existed over the years, including the West Bradford Women's Labour League, the Bradford branch of the Socialist Party, and the Bradford branch of the Women's Social & Political Union.

Alderman Kathleen Chambers was Bradford's first female lord mayor, who took office in 1945, in the wake of the Second World War. She was the latest in a line of women born in or associated with Bradford who made their mark in politics and public campaigning.

One of the best known of these women is Barbara Castle, the Labour Party MP who was educated at Bradford Girls' Grammar School and went on to hold several prestigious posts in Parliament. Perhaps Barbara was always destined to play a role in public life, since her family background gave her both the skills and the impetus to become involved in politics.

Barbara was born in Chesterfield in 1910, the daughter of Frank and Annie Betts, both of whom were passionate about politics. The Betts household must have been a fascinating place to grow up, and at the kitchen table both in Pontefract and Bradford, Barbara's childhood homes, she and her brother and sister would have listened to their parents discussing their activities – Frank edited the socialist *Bradford Pioneer* newspaper for a time after the family moved to Bradford in

1922, while Annie ran a soup kitchen for local miners. She would later become an MP herself.

It was at school that Barbara was really able to shine. Here, as a teenager, she honed the skills that would later stand her in good stead at Westminster. At an age when many girls were thinking about boys, clothes and trips to the cinema, Barbara presided at mock elections at school, posing as the Labour candidate, and also excelled at public speaking.

Some of Barbara's most long-lived achievements took place outside of our period, but are worth nothing as they still resonate in public life today – as Transport Minister in the late 1960s, Barbara brought in the breathalyser, the 70mph speed limit and the requirement that all new cars had to be fitted with a seat belt.

Barbara died in Chiltern, Buckinghamshire, at the age of 91, in 2002, having continued to be politically active until the end of her life. The Old Girls at Barbara's school award an annual statue named the Red Queen in her memory, to a girl who shows 'particular independence of spirit and mind'.

Bradford Spinsters' Pension Association

One of the city's most successful pressure groups, and one that made a difference on a national as well as a local level, was the Bradford Spinsters Pension Association, which was spearheaded by Florence White, who has a fascinating story. She went from mill girl to national campaigner and it's down to her guts and hard work that millions of UK women now collect a pension.

The National Spinsters' Association was founded in 1935 after a meeting in Bradford, and the group campaigned for pensions for women aged over 55. Many of those who joined the association were widows. Widows tended to be among the poorest in society and those too ill or too old to work could easily end up in the workhouse or dependent on the kindness of friends or on charity.

Many of these 'spinsters' were single not through choice but because of the huge losses in the male population due to the

First World War. Some 750,000 servicemen had been killed and millions of others were injured in what was called the war to end all wars. Spinsters tended to have to work in low-paid jobs and a large majority were working-class. Despite the negative connotations the word 'spinster' now has, in the Victorian and Edwardian era, and even beyond, many women were proud of being described as spinsters – independent, accountable to no one but themselves and making their own way in the world. Yet, spinsters were in a perilous position without a private income.

Florence White grew up in an industrial area in the Bowling district and would have been used to seeing women working alongside men in the mill, and then coming home to continue the work with their housework and families. Indeed, by the age of 12, Florence herself was working a twelve-hour day at Tankard's Mill. She had seen her mother ground down by the pressures of providing for Florence and her sister, as their father roamed the country, ostensibly working as an actor but sending little money home.

Enterprising Florence was a well-known figure around Bowling and Lidget Green, where she turned her skills to dressmaking after leaving the mill, and then set up a bakery. Florence is remarkable not only for taking the lead on this national issue, but also for the confidence and even humour with which she ran the campaign. Her publicity stunts, designed to draw positive attention to the cause, included presenting the prime minister, Neville Chamberlain, with an umbrella to protect spinsters for a 'rainy day' and encouraging every spinster to send the minister of health a Christmas card to keep the topic in his mind.

Typical of the jollity of the campaign was an event in August 1935, when a large outdoor meeting was held at Northcliffe Woods, between Manningham and Shipley, attended by eleven branches of the National Spinsters' Association. The event was an open-air rally and picnic tea but, typically for a British summer, rain arrived on the day. However, undeterred, the organisers ensured the event still went ahead. During the rally the women sang a song a weaver in Bramley had written:

Onward, spinsters, onward
Fight and you will win
if you get the pension
You have paid it in
Never look behind you,
always look before.
With Miss White as leader
You are sure to score.

There were speeches by representatives of different Yorkshire and Lancashire branches and, although apparently the Leeds contingent didn't like the connotations of the word spinster, they still took part enthusiastically. There had been a discussion over the name spinster, but the group concluded it originally meant 'one who spins', which was certainly nothing to be ashamed of. Northcliffe Woods was a popular walking and picnic spot and it's interesting to wonder what bystanders might have made of the singing and the gathering.

On the eve of the Second World War, the association had 125,000 members and almost a hundred branches around the country, with a million signatures gathered in support of the cause, an impressive number given that the total UK population was 47 million. Many married women were in fact supporters, knowing how easily their circumstances could change, leaving them without a source of income in their twilight years.

In 1940, the association received a partial victory with the Old Age and Widows' Pension Act, which meant pensions were awarded to all women at the age of 60 (but not 55 as the association had hoped). Then, in 1946, the National Insurance Act brought in the requirement for all working adults to make a state contribution in order to receive benefits, including unemployment, sickness and widow's benefit. Florence died in 1958 and is remembered by a plaque at 76 Kirkgate, where she made her first speech for the association.

Lady mayoresses

One way women could serve the community and raise money for charity was acting as lady mayoress, during the time that their husband was serving as lord mayor. Although the opportunities to shine on the public stage were many, with duties such as opening bazaars, attending public functions and handing out prizes, it is actually quite difficult to find information about these wives other than where they are mentioned as an adjunct or decorative part of their husband's work. For example, in 1934, the *Leeds Mercury* published a photo of Lady Mayoress Ella Hodgson under the headline 'she raised a smile' as she visited the children's ward at Bradford Royal Infirmary.

Another woman often mentioned was Mrs Jacob Moser (see Chapter 8), actually named Florence – the fact many of these women are named only by their husband's name shows what the times were like and the expectations of society, although Florence Moser did manage to make her own impact through her charity work.

It was not until 1945 that a female was appointed to the office of lord mayor, when Alderman Kathleen Chambers JP served in the post-war period 1945-46. It was during her time in office that a strange quirk of history happened. She was visiting Blenheim Terrace in Leeds on an appointment to the offices of the Northern Committees' Association of the Blind and her lord mayor's chain of office had been left in the civic car in a concealed briefcase. A thief or thieves managed to gain access to the car and the briefcase was taken. Despite a wide-ranging call for information, the lord mayor's chain was never recovered and although three men were convicted, one of whom was jailed, the chain had been broken up after the theft.

Former Lord Mayor Alderman William Illingworth called upon the people of Bradford to donate any gold items such as jewellery they could spare to be melted down into a replacement chain. He was not disappointed by the response, as people around the city responded with generosity, making sufficient donations for the 100oz needed. Fattorini & Sons Ltd made the splendid replacement in their Birmingham workshops, and this chain was used until 1977, with an inscription on the back explaining how it came to be made.

Political societies and associations

Women could make a difference without having to go to the lengths of becoming a politician or staging a campaign by joining a society association for the political party to which they belonged. The Conservative, Labour and Liberal parties all had women's branches in Bradford over the years. However, certainly at the start of the life of such associations, women were often relegated to stereotypical female roles such as organising fundraising bazaars, manning the stalls and providing and serving refreshments.

There was also the social side, with women being able to add their voices to various political campaigns.

CHAPTER FIVE

Working Life

❖

The women of Bradford have long been able to, and have often had little choice but to, turn their hand to part-time or full-time jobs, as well as managing a home and often caring for a family.

The textile trade is examined in detail in Chapter 7, so in this chapter we'll look largely at non-textile occupations. West Yorkshire differed from many UK regions and counties in its employment patterns as there were few stately homes in or around the city. In towns and villages with one or more 'big house' that had an aristocratic family in residence, literally hundreds of local people would be employed on the estate and in the house, many of whom would receive bed and board or tied accommodation as part of their employment package. Whole families could be employed, for example with the woman of a family as the housekeeper, her husband as gardener, and teenage children working in service at the same house.

This type of set up was rare in Bradford. The big houses that existed tended not to have extensive grounds, and the number of staff employed in even the biggest of these houses would run into the dozens rather than the hundreds. The grand houses constructed during the Industrial Revolution in areas such as Manningham and Frizinghall did have live-in accommodation for a maid or two. But on the whole, Bradford remained less an employer of domestic staff than other towns and rural areas, where a stately home was a major employer. Statistics for the UK in 1911 show an average of 170 servants per 1,000 families, yet in the West Riding of Yorkshire the figure was only 100 per 1,000 families.

In Bradford and many other West Riding towns, servants preferred to live out rather than in, for more freedom, leisure time and the chance to pursue hobbies and relationships outside of working hours. When there was an opportunity to earn money in a mill or shop and be free to return home at the end of the day, most would prefer to do this rather than being at the beck and call of an employer if they lived in. The First World War also saw women recruited into munitions factories, such as that at Low Moor, with many leaving service to do so, and the majority of these women would never return to domestic service with many able to move into work previously reserved for men.

Newspapers such as the *Bradford Observer* and *Yorkshire Post* carried pages full of adverts of servants wanted and servants seeking positions, as well as situations for teachers and governesses. These adverts often state what other servants are employed at the house, the duties to be carried out, and where the family lived, as well as specifics such as wage and other inducements, such as free time and holidays.

The *Yorkshire Post & Leeds Intelligencer* of 28 August 1885 carried the following advertisement:

> Wanted, thoroughly good plain cook; good bread maker and able to manage small dairy and make butter. Kitchen maid kept.

Applicants had to write to Mrs Tom Mitchell of The Park, Eccleshill. The same page asked for a general servant able to do washing, offering an £18 annual wage, for a family in St Mary's Road, Manningham.

Education played a big part in the options that were open to working women. And women of all classes were susceptible to the pressures of society and family when it came to taking on work, with religion, tradition and economic circumstances playing their part.

Teaching or tutoring was one option for wealthy and middle-class women, as the Brontë sisters Charlotte and Anne, in nearby

Haworth, had famously proved not long before the start of this period. These two women, who would achieve worldwide fame as novelists along with their sister Emily, had both worked as governesses for wealthy families and this employment was seen as suitable for the intelligent daughters of a respected clergyman. The *Yorkshire Post* of 26 July 1938 asked for a school-leaver to train as a governess in a 'good boarding school', and on 28 June 1940, the same paper asked for a 'nursery-governess' for the Shipley area who was fond of country life and willing to help care for children and run a house, where two maids were also employed.

Teachers and governesses could also advertise their services in local newspapers, which would be full of 'position wanted' notices, with would-be employees setting out their accomplishments, such as music and dancing tuition, or experience with very young children. Many of these women would have been well educated and often well-travelled, if what they told potential employers in their advert was true. Such an education would have been the product of a wealthy background, as in the case of a 'young lady' who wrote to the *Bradford Observer* on 19 December 1867 stating she was looking for employment as a governess in the Bradford district and, as well as teaching English, had experience of French – 'acquired during a residence on the Continent' – and also music and drawing. We can only imagine the boasting that might have gone on in the drawing room in a well-to-do area of Bradford: 'Oh yes, this is our new governess, just returned from a stay on the Continent …'

Shop work

Shop work ranged from work in a local corner shop, which was often temporary or part-time, through to employment in one of the city's big department stores or shopping arcades, many of which were frequented by wealthy customers who expected high standards of service and a wide choice of luxury goods.

Although shop work didn't necessarily require formal qualifications, the ability to carry out rapid mental arithmetic and basic reading and writing skills were essential, as were customer care skills. Jobs in the smaller shops were often advertised purely by word of mouth or by a card placed in the shop window inviting applicants to call inside.

For larger shops, applicants would have been expected to attend a more formal interview, usually after applying for the position through an employment agency or newspaper advert. Even during the Second World War, demand for luxury goods was such that department store Brown Muffs placed an advert asking for experienced practical women furriers, while in 1940, the store asked for an 'experienced young lady' aged between 20-22 for its 'high class' millinery department.

A number of large department stores were established in Bradford, as well as the much-admired and beautifully decorated Swan Arcade, which opened in 1880 opposite the Wool Exchange. These kinds of stores, which catered mainly for wealthy and middle-class women, were arranged into different departments, many of which sold luxurious goods such as furs, jewellery, made-to-measure ballgowns and sumptuous fabrics for dressmaking.

A woman who worked at such a store would, at first glance, seem to have a superior working environment, compared, for example, to a mill or a small, draughty corner shop. However, the hours could be long and customers were demanding, especially in an environment with wealthy shoppers used to staff attending on their beck and call, and a place where the customer was 'always right'.

Busby's on Manningham Lane was known for treating its staff well and for its family atmosphere and its tagline 'the store with the friendly welcome'. A 1942 newspaper advert invited applications for the post of window dresser, which was open to men and women, offering a 'liberal salary' and hours from 8.30 a.m. to 5.30 p.m.

And it wasn't just on the shop floor that work could be had. The vacancies columns of newspapers of this period carry

Above: *Textile mills dominated the skyline at the height of the textile trade. (© Tim Green)*

Below: *Heaton Mount, once a grand family home in Manningham and now part of the University of Bradford. (© Tim Green)*

Above: *Kirkgate Market, a favourite with generations of shoppers.*

Below left: *Cockle Sarah.*

Below right: *Wealthy girls were largely taught at home in the 19th century.*

Above left: *Statue of W.E. Forster. (© Tim Green)*

Above right: *English Heritage plaque commemorating Rachel and Margaret McMillan at their lodging place on Tweedy Road, Bromley. (© Spudgun67)*

Saltaire Institute.
(© Tim Green)

Brooch in the suffragette colours of white, purple and green. (© Glasgow Women's Library)

SUFFRAGETTE PROCESSION JUNE 17, 1911.

SHIPLEY GLEN, BRADFORD.

Above: *1911 Suffragette procession in London. (© Library of Congress. George Bain Collection)*

Left: *Shipley Glen, scene of a mass votes for women rally in 1908. (© Tuck D.B. Postcards)*

Above: *Suffragette placard procession,*
(© Library of Congress, George Bain.
Collection)

Right: *Barbara Castle pictured in 1965.*
(© National Archives of Malawi)

Above: *National Spinsters' Association campaigners. (© West Yorkshire Archive Service, Bradford ref 78D86/4/3)*

Below: *Bradford Town Hall, the seat of office of the city's Lord Mayor and Lady Mayoress. (© Tuck D.B. Postcards)*

Above left: *An Edwardian postcard celebrating Bradford's beautiful women. (© Tuck D.B. Postcards)*

Above right: *Once women had children they were often out of the workforce.*

Right: *Novels such as Charles Dickens' Oliver Twist portrayed the workhouse as a place to be feared.*

MANNINGHAM MILLS STRIKE
CENTENARY
1890   1990
At this place in
December 1890 began the
Manningham Mills Strike,
which lasted until April
1891. This led to the
founding of the Bradford
Labour Union which in
turn saw the formation of
the national Independent
Labour Party in Bradford
three years later.

Bradford City Heritage

Above left: *The Holme on Thornton Road, built in 1798 and reputedly Bradford's first factory.*

Above right: *The chimney at Lister's Mill. Generations of Bradford people have grown up hearing the tale that the top of the chimney was wide enough to take a horse and cart.*

Left: *Plaque commemorating the Manningham Mills Strike of 1890–1891. (© Tim Green)*

Above: *Salts Mill, once a village at the heart of Bradford's textile industry and now a World Heritage Site. (© Tim Green)*

Below: *Memorial to those killed in the Newlands Mill disaster.*

Above: *Bradford Forster Square, the first sight of Bradford for immigrants arriving in the city by train.*

Below left: *Drawing of migrants arriving by ship after a long and crowded sea journey. (© Library of Congress)*

Below right: *Australian poster inviting people to start a new life in a new country. (© Library of Congress)*

THE STARS WHICH SHINE
OVER AUSTRALIA
THE LAND OF
OPPORTUNITY

THE "SOUTHERN CROSS"

THE CALL OF THE STARS TO BRITISH MEN & WOMEN

★ MEN FOR THE LAND
★ WOMEN FOR THE HOME
★ EMPLOYMENT GUARANTEED
★ GOOD WAGES
★ PLENTY OF OPPORTUNITY

FOR FURTHER INFORMATION APPLY TO ANY EMPLOYMENT EXCHANGE
OR TO THE DIRECTOR OF MIGRATION AND SETTLEMENT.
AUSTRALIA HOUSE, STRAND, W.C.2.

Above left: *Poster for the Division for Foreign Born Women, which supported female US immigrants. (© Library of Congress)*

Above right: *Nurse Mitchell, matron of Sir Titus Salt Hospital in the First World War.*

Below: *Women's Canteen at Phoenix Works, Bradford – painting by Flora Lion. (© Imperial War Museums)*

Above: *Low Moor Ironworks.*

Below: *Peel Park pictured in 1916.*

Above: *Crowds at Bowling Tide, early twentieth century. (© East Bowling History Group)*

Right: *Allerton's war memorial is relatively unusual in featuring a female figure.*

VICARAGE ENTRANCE, BOWLING PARK.

Miss
Gertie
Milla

1689

Above: *Bowling Park in 1916.*

Left: *Edwardian theatre star Gertie Millar.*

Above: *Scene from the 1931 Bradford Pageant.*

Below: *City Hall.*

*Bradford
Cathedral.
(© Tim Green)*

Judy Barrett.

regular shop vacancies for shops such as Busby's, but other, more varied, work could also be on offer, including clerical positions within these big stores, such as in the wages office, as a secretary or typist and, in the case of the successful applicant to a position advertised in January 1938, the librarian of a new department to be set up at Busby's. The 'experienced librarian' was invited to apply by post, giving details of the salary he or she expected, with the assurance that applications were strictly confidential.

Brown Muff's was a drapery, opened in 1814 by Elizabeth Brown at 11 Market Street, which was so successful that, by 1822, it was also a library and bookshop. Elizabeth retired in 1834, after when her son Henry ran the shop, which thrived when the trains reached Bradford in 1846, bringing in customers from the outlying suburbs and further afield. The store even had an advertisement window in Forster Square Station in which they could display their latest wares to tempt customers to visit their five floors of luxury goods before going to any other shop.

An 1856 trade directory lists Brown Muff's as drapers, tailors, hosiers and hatters. The store opened a beauty parlour in 1927, but fell victim to the depression years of the early 1930s and widened its product range, even selling the Women's Voluntary Services uniform during the Second World War. Brown Muff's closed in 1995, when it became part of House of Fraser.

Sunwin House, on Sunbridge Road, was built in 1935 and opened in 1936. Its striking Thirties design made it a landmark for decades, and it is now classed as a Grade II listed building. Like other department stores, Sunwin House employed hundreds of women over the years in roles ranging from café attendant to beauty hall assistant. The premises were originally named the City of Bradford Co-operative Society, with a large sign proclaiming so. This society, said a poster of the time, was the creation of the citizens of Bradford over four generations. The achievement of ordinary men and women.

As well as the usual departments where a female shopworker might hope to find employment, such as clothing, hairdressing and the food hall, there was also a funeral service, travel agent, laundry section and dispensing, all under one roof.

For many years, the windows of Sunwin House were eagerly anticipated for their Christmas display, with dozens of Christmas trees on display, eagerly spotted by children on buses heading into the city, or out towards suburbs such as Saltaire and Shipley.

Casual work

Not all women were employed on a formal basis, or even received payment for their services. Across the city, neighbours helped each other on an informal basis, for example, babysitting local children when a parent was at work, helping a mother give birth to a child and making clothes for those who didn't have the necessary skills. And, of course, the old saying that a woman's work is never done held true at home, with countless women returning from a shift at work to begin another job at home, the labour of love of caring for a home and family.

Some female family members cared for dependants in households other than their own, for example acting as an unpaid carer for an ailing parent or helping a son or daughter with the grandchildren. Many of these acts have gone unrecorded, remaining only in the folklore of family stories and, in some cases, in obituaries – although these tended to be restricted to those with the means to place a newspaper notice after a death.

Over the years, thousands of the city's women have volunteered their services to charity work, helping in soup kitchens, volunteering at church bazaars, making donations to appeals and sewing clothes for soldiers away at war, is a topic explored in more depth in Chapter 6. The pages of local newspapers often carried reports of charitable social events, particularly those that ran over several days, such as a charity bazaar in November 1901 to aid the children's hospital, which was given a column in the *Yorkshire Post* that explained £3,000 of funding was needed to create an isolation ward. The ambitiously staged event promised a Chinese pagoda tower, a thatched cottage for the sale of game, eggs and butter, and 'quaintly tricked out' dairymaids selling their wares.

Wealthy working women

Despite the fact that any advances in education might have made women more employable, many firms were reluctant to employ married women. Indeed, until as late as the 1970s, some organisations encouraged married women to work only until they were pregnant with their first child.

Women who didn't need the money, because they received an allowance from the family or had their own private means, often occupied themselves with charity work. Some of this work, such as the token attendance on a charity committee, was more or less done for social purposes. However, many women were physically active in helping to better the lives of others, such as volunteers with Bradford's Guild of Help, who called on those in need and offered advice and practical assistance.

Differences between employment for men and women

For men and women around the UK there were marked discrepancies in employment, mostly in terms of wages. This problem was particularly acute in Bradford because of the textile trade. Women carried out the tasks that paid less. It wasn't that men and women were doing the same jobs but being paid at different rates (as is sometimes the case even today), but more that women worked in areas of the textile trade that paid less.

This pattern can also be observed in other fields of work including shop work and office work. Lack of childcare and the expectation that once women married and had children, they were out of the workforce was another reason many women worked in low-paid and monotonous jobs. Today's nursery and childminder network didn't exist on a large enough scale to benefit women. Working-class women would often return to work only at times when the need for money was acute, perhaps after the death of an older relative whose funeral needed to be paid for, or maybe when saving up to move house or buy new furniture.

Even wealthier women of the middle and upper classes found large sectors of the working world closed to them. Of course, there were some exceptions, such as the headmistress of

Bradford Girl's Grammar School, and pioneering women such as Julia Varley and Margaret McMillan, but these people were very much out of the ordinary. And the rarity of their work is one reason we know so much about them.

Women could keep inns, taverns and hotels under their own name, whether single, married or widowed. In 1851, in the Borough of Bradford, there were 101 innkeepers and 135 licensed victuallers, and the wives of innkeepers and victuallers were listed separately because their contribution was significant. Many times, a husband recorded another occupation on the census as well, and his wife is not listed as the licensee, although it's clear she probably ran the inn or beerhouse.

Evidence for what working life was like

One of the best ways to discover what life was like for working women is to hear or read their words from the substantial collection held at Bradford Local Studies Library. This project, carried out in the 1980s, saw hundreds of women (and men) interviewed about many different aspects of their lives, including working conditions, the expectations of society when it came to working outside the home, and the age-old challenge of juggling work and home life and children.

These interviews give an interesting insight into a way of life now gone forever:

> We'd no wash basins, they used to have a bucket of water in the middle of the aisle with a tablet of soap, and you'd to wash your hands in there. Some of the young boys would think nothing of getting a dead mouse and dropping that in, and there'd be ladies screaming all over the place.

> There was no conversation as such, and it was how you learned to lip read, and you could speak to each other over the top of the frames. But if you were caught talking too much you were told about it in no uncertain terms. But you had to do something. Fortunately for us

the rhythm of the belt and the machinery would start off a song, and it would create another one and we would sing nearly all day long. (F, born 1924.)

I worked half time. I went to school in the morning and into the mill in the afternoon, and I got two-and-nine pence one week and three-and-nine the following week. I went by myself to this mill. I knew they'd set me on. But you'd to go to the Town Hall, and if you hadn't so many attendances at school you couldn't go half time. … Half-past-five, get up make a fire, make a cup of tea, go to the mill for six o'clock and come back at quarter-past-eight for another cup of tea. Go back at half past eight and then come home at half past twelve for my dinner … And I did that till I was thirteen and then I left school altogether and went to work full-time. And I got nine-and-six a week then. But the mill, when you're a little girl of 12, to get up at half-past-five every morning is a poor life for a girl. (F, born 1900.)

You couldn't get past as the flow [of people] covered all the pavements and the road. There was a siren at lunchtime and evening to signal the end of work. (Mary Sowden.)

The evidence for wages can be hard to find, since many jobs for women were found by word of mouth with no written contracts. However, the job adverts of local newspapers and magazines can give some idea of what a job entailed and how much it paid. Certain outside influences, such as war, brought more women into the workplace and there are registers relating to this. There were also some employment bureaux, such as for the textile trade.

Some people made a living from helping others to find work, much in the way that a recruitment industry would today. The domestic service industry was ideal for such a state of affairs, although domestic service was much less prevalent in Bradford with a well-paid textile industry offering wages and a certain amount of freedom compared to those who lived in as a maid or servant.

Wages and working conditions

Textile work was considered to be relatively well-paid compared to other jobs for women (see also Chapter 7), although the wage-gap between men and women could be considerable. Elsewhere, it was a case of finding a job that fitted in with family life and household duties, as few women had the option of working outside the home while paid staff looked after their house.

Some work was seasonal. Mill-work in particular could go into short-time or lay workers off during times of hardship. It could be the same in other industries as few people were working on a contract. This did, however, mean it was easy to move from one place of work to another without a long period of notice. The saying 'chasing the sixpence' comes from the textile industry and refers to a person who moved from one mill to another in search of better pay.

There were several periods of depression: In the 1880s, around the time of the formation of the Independent Labour Party in the 1890s, the slump following the First World War and also the late 1920s/early 1930s. Many women were at the sharp end of such depressions, either through losing the income of their husband or father who was the main wage-earner, or perhaps being laid-off or put on short-time themselves. At times, women filled in the gap left by men, for example while soldiers were fighting in the First World War, but were then expected to give up their job and go back to home life when the men returned.

CHAPTER SIX

Poverty and Charity

❖

Bradford was a place with severe health issues that affected people of all classes and ages. Just a couple of years before our period begins, a cholera epidemic killed hundreds of people and 800 of those victims lay buried in St Paul's Churchyard in Manningham, some of whom were laid to rest just streets from where they had lived in squalid and insanitary conditions.

The town may have been buoyant in terms of industry and inventions, but the huge population boom that had provided the labour to run the city's industries had a pay-off – the population exploded and public health facilities and services simply hadn't kept pace, particularly when it came to housing and sanitation.

The 1848 cholera outbreak in the UK brought in a Public Health Act later that year that allowed for the supply of fresh water, the removal of waste from dwellings, improved drainage and provision of sewers, and the appointment of a medical officer for each town. Despite the good intentions of the act, the responsibility for each of the provisions was optional, meaning that officials could plead lack of funds and, thus, not follow through on their responsibilities.

POVERTY

Poor provision and public health

Over the centuries, the UK has tried many ways of dealing with the poor, some schemes more successful than others. Before the Industrial Revolution, poor relief was largely dealt with by individual parishes, with those in need being the responsibility of the parish where they lived or were born. With the Victorian age came the Poor Law, and with it the dreaded workhouse, which caught the public's imagination through novelists such as Charles Dickens, who wrote *Oliver Twist*, the heart-rending tale of an orphaned boy who escaped workhouse life to begin again in London.

The Poor Law riots of the mid-1830s fall outside the period of our Bradford women. However, it is interesting to note what happened as it explains how women were affected. The 'new' Poor Law of 1834 replaced a system that had been in place since the late sixteenth century. Under the new system, those in need were no longer to be cared for by individual parishes, but a national system would operate, administered by Poor Law Unions where those without the means to care for themselves (e.g. the unemployed or elderly) would enter the workhouse and receive board and lodgings in exchange for carrying out manual tasks, and abide by the strict rules of the institution.

Going into the workhouse was seen as a very last resort, and many people would pawn or sell their possessions or even take to the road to avoid it. It was a place where families were split up and men, women and children housed separately, regardless of family groupings. Harsh measures, such as workhouse uniforms, unpleasant tasks and a monotonous diet, were put into place to deter people from entering the system unless they truly were in desperate need.

The system began to decline after the reign of Queen Victoria, from the start of the twentieth century, as Liberal reforms brought about differences to the welfare system, and extra protection came in to aid workers, such as trade unionism as well as the work of charities and friendly societies.

Bradford's first workhouse was built well before the New Poor Law, in 1738 in the north-east of the town at Barkers End, and was named the Bradford Union Workhouse, taking in both male and female 'vagrants'. It was rebuilt in 1790 to an 'L-shaped' plan, with separate wings for men and women, meaning that families would be split up on entering the institution.

The Bradford Poor Law Union came into being on 10 February 1837 with thirty-two guardians representing twenty parishes. In the same year, troops from both Leeds and London were despatched to Bradford to deal with anti-poor law rioters, with crowds of up to 1,000 reported. Little Horton Workhouse was built, opening in 1851 and described in a local directory as 'spacious, handsome and admirably arranged'.

Within just a year of opening, two of the workhouse staff had been accused of neglect, causing the death of an inmate, and the workhouse master had been suspended for 'habitual drunkenness and immoral conduct', with another male member of staff dismissed for 'improper connection' with a female inmate.

It was at this workhouse in 1901 that a change in dietary regulations caused a mutiny, led by a group of women who behaved in a 'rowdy manner' and ended up in jail for their pains. This time the incident was actually not the fault of those in charge. The dietary regulations had come in from government level, instructing that workhouse inhabitants were to be served gruel rather than tea.

No one comes between an Englishman or woman and their cup of tea, as this incident would prove. When presented with a cup of glutinous liquid instead of the strongly brewed cuppa they were used to, the women rose up and left the room. The situation turned into a work to rule strike, with the ringleaders encouraging others not to do any more work until the decision was reversed. Alas, three of the rebels were rounded up and sent to court, where they were condemned to a week in jail.

When it comes to workhouse inmates and staff, the census shines an interesting spotlight onto who resided in the workhouse at a given day on a particular year. For example, the 1881 census for the Bradford Union Workhouse has details of workhouse master John Heap and his wife Mary Ann, both aged 54 and from Derby. Working alongside them were a team of fifteen, including a cook, porter, schoolmaster, schoolmistress and several lunatic attendants, the youngest of whom was 22-year-old Annie Foulks from Manchester.

The inmates were aged from 2 months to 86 years, from a range of trades. A sample of the women's trades includes cotton spinner, charwoman, domestic servant, seamstress and cook. Although many are recorded as being Bradford-born, others hailed from Ireland, Lancashire and the south of England, perhaps having arrived in Bradford for work and then falling victim to a dip in trade or the loss of the family breadwinner.

A Long Life

In March 1920, a redoubtable lady named Mary Brannan died at the age of 106, having spent the final seventeen years of her life in Bowling Park Workhouse. She attributed her long life to 'a bit o'good baccy'.

Bradford Orphan Girls' Home

A less forbidding place than the workhouse, and one that helped dozens of Bradford girls over the decades, was the Bradford Orphan Girls Home, which opened in 1865 in Roberts Place with just three girls. It moved to Brunswick Place and expanded to offer places for twenty girls. The home was intended to provide shelter for children from the workhouse, but eventually admitted anyone whose place was paid for by a friend or relative. The year after the home opened there was an explosion at a colliery in Barnsley that left several children homeless, and some of the girls who lost family members in the accident were transferred to this home.

On 14 April 1871, bigger premises opened on Manningham Lane (on a section of the road that later became Keighley Road). With typical Victorian paternalism and practicality, the girls were trained for work in the outside world with skills such as baking, cooking, sewing and cleaning, and they could stay at the home until the age of 16. It was optimistically called 'a most desirable and cheerful residence' by the

Bradford Observer, who also noted the plain and functional decoration.

The home does seem to have stayed in the minds of those who opened and ran it, with reports of Christmas meals and presents donated over the years, as well as visitors to the home at various times. An annual meeting was held for decades, often presided over by the mayor and mayoress of the city. One name mentioned in the records as a benefactor is Mrs Cutcliffe Hyne of Heaton Lodge, wife of the author C.J. Cutcliffe Hyne, whose only son was killed in the First World War.

In 1926, the girls' home was renamed St Hilda's Home for Girls and re-opened on 5 October 1927 by Princess Mary (who lived at Harewood House, one of Bradford's nearest stately homes). Under the new regime, the girls had their own girl guides group and even a percussion band, which was set up following a visit from a musician. The girls' voices could be heard on two gramophone records that were recorded when they went on a trip to the Albert Hall in London with Mr S. Moore, honorary secretary of the Worcestershire Musical Association. The orphan girls were evacuated to Rhyl in 1939 and seem never to have returned. The home then passed into private use.

Kate Pickard

One of the city's well-loved benefactresses was Kate Pickard who, at the time of her death in January 1953, had been associated with Bradford Cathedral for 77 years. She was the founder, with Dr Margaret Sharp, of St Monica's Home, and also opened a commercial school for women in the early 1900s, allowing her students to learn the skills required for clerical work. She lived at Nesfield House on Nesfield Street, not far from where Midland Hotel stands.

HEALTH

At the turn of the twentieth century, Bradford had the second highest infant mortality rate in Britain. The town was still one of the most polluted in Britain and, even on the eve of the First World War, a report by the medical officer for the City of Bradford 1913 said: 'At this stage of pregnancy [later pregnancy] malnutrition in the mother and inappropriate work such as factory labour have the most potent effect upon the wellbeing of the coming child.'

Health care in the UK wasn't free or universally available. Within living memory good health was sometimes the province only of those who could afford it. Private doctors and nurses, maternity clinics and alternative practitioners were all available only to those who could afford to pay for them, and these occupations provided many with a living.

However, for lots of ordinary people, health care, including issues such as childbirth, was provided by knowledgeable friends and neighbours, a local doctor prepared to help for a reduced fee, or by an institution such as the Bradford Children's Hospital in Manningham, opened in 1889 and run by All Saints Sisterhood.

Morley Street Health Centre was another such facility, with health visitors and midwives to help poorer mothers. And Bradford Royal Infirmary has helped generations of Bradfordians. There was also the charmingly named Tired Mothers Holiday Club, which was available to those in need, with a holiday home in Addingham, on the outskirts of the Yorkshire Dales, providing much needed respite for hard-pressed urban mothers.

The city's efforts on the health front were recognised in October 1925, when the minister of health, Neville Chamberlain, visited Bradford, with his wife, and officially opened a new thoroughfare, named Neville Road. The six-hour inspection tour included St Luke's Hospital, an anti-tuberculosis unit, the White Abbey Improvement Area, and housing estates, followed by a private lunch at the town hall. The minister pronounced himself glad to hear that slum areas would soon be cleared and is said to have particularly admired the Central Infant Welfare Centre.

In November 1928, a birth control van was burnt-out by a woman named Elizabeth Ellis of Thornton. The van belonged to the Constructive Birth Control Society, whose president was Marie Stopes.

The arsonist was identified as a confectioner's assistant, aged 34, who was sent to prison for two months. The defence called her 'a woman of high ideals and religious temperament' who had a poor start in life, but when standing by the caravan 'became indignant at the conversation she heard among the young people around her. She said the society's literature was 'filthy and pornographic' and would encourage immorality and prostitution.

CHARITY

Societies

One of the best-known charitable organisations is the Cinderella Club, formed in 1890 originally to provide hot meals to children living in poverty, and eventually rolling out to help children across Bradford through initiatives and activities including the provision of clothing and shoes, day trips and its well-known Hest Bank holiday camp near Morecambe, which could take up to forty children at a time between April and October, giving youngsters the chance to enjoy a fortnight of sea air, beach jaunts and home-cooked food. According to the club's official history, children could come home from their two-week break half a stone heavier than when they had arrived, presumably also full of tales of the fun they'd had.

During the Second World War, Hest Bank took on a new life as a home for refugees, while back in Bradford, the club came to the aid of families struggling financially with the main breadwinner away in the armed forces. So successful and well set up was the club that, during the depression years of the late 1920s and early 1930s, the city council appealed to the club for its assistance in reaching out to those in need.

Helen Priscilla McLaren Rabagliati MBE

Born in 1851 in Edinburgh, Helen Priscilla was a bright and forthright advocate of women's rights, health improvements and education. She was the daughter of Scottish Liberal politician Duncan McLaren and Priscilla Bright, and niece of John Bright, co-founder of the Anti-Corn Law league.

Helen's work was hands-on. She helped found both St Catherine's hospice and St Monica's maternity home in Bradford. During her early married life, she was a Manningham resident, moving later to Ben Rhydding to live in a house named Whinbrae with her surgeon husband, Dr Andrea Carlo Francisco Rabagliati.

Helen died in 1934 and her funeral was attended by representatives of the Mother's Union and women's Conservative associations. According to her funeral elegy, she had a low tolerance of anyone who was purely pleasure seeking.

Bradford City Guild of Help

Bradford City Guild of Help was a well-regarded charity that tried to alleviate poverty and encourage people to help themselves. However, in many ways it was just as much of a help to those who volunteered as to those for whom the aid was intended. Its motto 'not alms but a friend' had a no-nonsense but friendly feel and, from its foundation in 1904, the organisation aimed to get its clients either state or charity assistance to help them get back on their feet. Within a year of operations, it had 500 helpers and 2,000 people in need of help on its books. The aid tended not to be money but things like clothes, or practical assistance such as getting free school meals for children. Casual work was a big cause of poverty and this could be prevalent in the textile trade, where such situations accounted for up to twenty per cent of guild cases.

The guild's area of operations was divided into four divisions based on the established Poor Law administration areas, meaning that it could offer assistance in a precise and efficient manner. People could apply for help directly or someone such as a doctor or priest could make a request on their behalf. In order to help with public health education, the guild ran themed 'health weeks' to draw attention to issues such as tuberculosis. It also ran baby clinics, where parents could call in on an informal basis for advice on matters such as growth and nutrition.

Many of the guild's helpers were young unmarried women from the middle and upper classes – people such as Helen Lister, daughter of textile baron Samuel Cunliffe Lister. This type of work was seen as socially acceptable for wealthier women, both before and after marriage.

Another such woman was Emily Wright, born in Bradford in 1882, the daughter of a barrister. Emily wanted to enter law but, because women couldn't become lawyers at this time, she volunteered with the Bradford City Guild of Help. Despite the fact that many women made up the volunteer force, all the main division heads of the guild were men – and an issue of its in-house magazine *Help* in 1906 reported that 152 helpers were men and 222 women.

Martha Leach

Born in 1876, Martha Leach married Bradford worsted manufacturer William Leach and became a philanthropist and social reformer. She visited Bradford slums to give practical help to their inhabitants and she replaced Margaret McMillan on the Bradford School Board in 1902. She also became the first female member of Bradford Education Committee in 1920, serving until 1955.

In 1946, Martha acted as lady mayoress for Kathleen Chambers (another woman had to act as lady mayoress if a woman was the mayor, rather than having a man perform the secondary role). In the course of her work, Martha met many interesting and well-known people including MP Ramsay Macdonald, author and philosopher Bertrand Russell, and MP Norman Angell.

However, her work wasn't all about public appearances. She could give practical help when called upon. For example, she housed the children of miners during industrial strikes and gave accommodation to unemployed speakers visiting Bradford.

St Monica's Rescue Maternity Home

'No girl is ever refused help' was the hearty motto of St Monica's Rescue Maternity Home at Belle Vue which, at its peak, helped a thousand of the city's young women, many of whom had been abandoned by their families.

In 1939, a report in the *Yorkshire Post* said that 883 girls had been cared for the year previously, including a girl of just 13 who'd given birth to a boy at the home. The matron, Miss Emily Southworth, explained that the girls 'did well' after leaving if they were just shown some kindness.

CHARITY

For some women, although social pressures or their own choice may have prevented them from working for charitable purposes, leaving money in a will was another way to support a cause. Other women might give to a charity, such as the Lord Mayor's Appeal, or contribute goods to a charity bazaar or appeal. The Bradford's Lord Mayor's Appeal is a long-running charity which, over the years, has given to a variety of different causes. Seeing how the causes supported have changed over the decades is a fascinating way to understand what issues were supported and what social pressures communities were facing.

For example, during the Second World War, citizens were encouraged to contribute towards the comforts of soldiers serving on the Front. In the First World War, practical citizens donated packets of cigarettes to the troops, which the lord mayor gamely promised to deliver in person to York.

Florence Moser

On 2 July 1960, the *Telegraph & Argus* reported on 'Couple who gave away over £300,000'. Florence Moser was born around 1856 in Manchester. In 1898 she and her husband Jacob Moser gave £10,000 to form a 'benevolent fund for the aged and infirm workpeople of Bradford' and then, in 1908, donated £5,000 to Bradford Royal Infirmary Fund.

Florence opened The Nest in Westgate where, for a small charge, working mothers could leave babies and infants in their care to be fed and looked after from 8 a.m. to 6 p.m. This ran for around twenty-five years. She also established the Bradford City Guild of Help.

On 27 October 1911, *Bradford Weekly Telegraph* reported that Florence had been on Bradford Board of Guardians for Workhouse for around nine years and had been one of a few fellow guardians 'practically responsible for many reforms at the workhouse', making sure that properly qualified nurses were employed and that married couples could be cared for together.

Charity concerts and bazaars

One of the most popular ways of raising money was via events such as charity concerts and bazaars. While many female charity workers got stuck into the less glamorous side of charity work, such as prison visits, calls to impoverished families and serving in soup kitchens, for other women another option was to help organise a concert or run a bazaar, perhaps helping on one of the stalls or overseeing the whole event.

Charity bazaars were a popular way to raise money for different causes, particularly in the days before the National Health Service (NHS) brought in healthcare for all. A bazaar held at St George's Hall in November 1911 received a column-long write-up in the *Yorkshire Post & Leeds Intelligencer*, which said it had been organised on an 'elaborate scale' to raise money for the Bradford Children's Hospital, with an event that ran for a week. The Mayor of Bradford opened proceedings on day one, with Lady Powell doing the honours the following day and the Countess of Warwick the day after that. The event would certainly have been something to remember, with a thatched cottage containing poultry, a Chinese pagoda from which flowers were sold, and costumed performers milling around the stalls, including children in 'cherry ripe' dresses, 'quaintly tricked out' dairymaids, and nurses dressed in blue.

One of the city's most high-profile fundraising bazaars, for the Liberal Party, ran from 28 to 31 March 1928 at the Windsor Halls on Morley Street. At the outset, it was stated that the event needed £10,000 'to make Bradford liberalism independent of any outside funds'. The opening ceremony was carried out by Miss Megan Lloyd George.

The bazaar programme lists dozens of women working on the stalls, serving home produce, ice cream, and high teas and suppers until as late as 10 p.m. There were home-cooked goods, such as sausage and mash and steak and kidney pie, and customers could enjoy music from the Sunbeam Band while they dined.

Big changes

Anyone in the town around 1860 would have seen some very big changes taking place as the town moved from being a rural market settlement to a major commercial centre of trade and manufacture, and poor people were often at the sharp end of such change.

For example, slums were knocked down at Sunbridge Road, Godwin Street and Grattan Road, old coaching inns where coaches and horses would have called in with their passengers were disappearing and being replaced by new buildings. Life was becoming more organised as neighbourhoods took shape, churches, social societies, friendly societies and even a main sewer system were all put into place.

The number of professional people and their families entering Bradford doubled between 1860 and 1880, with houses for solicitors, doctors, engineers and teachers, now catered for with numerous fine homes being built on what had, for many generations, been farmland.

CHAPTER SEVEN

The Textile Trade

✦

The words 'Bradford' and 'textiles' have long been entwined and many volumes have been written about the trade, its history and the world domination. There must be few Bradford families who don't have a historic connection with the trade, either through an ancestor who worked in textiles or someone employed in one of the ancillary industries.

Bradford women have worked in textiles for as long as the industry has existed. Before the start of our period, for women, textile work had been available as a home-working occupation, to be carried out alongside other family members and in between other household chores. Although the work could be repetitive and poorly paid, it at least had the advantage of allowing women to pick up and drop the work as and when needed, without the tie of working for an employer at a workplace. Also, older children could take their turn in doing some of the work should the need arise. What no one could have known is that within the space of less than a generation, a textile revolution was on the horizon that would change production methods beyond anything anyone could have imagined.

Textile production had moved largely onto a factory-based system and, as mechanisation brought home-working to an end and the focus shifted to factories, many women got caught up in the cycle of low-paid work at an unpleasant workplace in unhealthy conditions, often working for a harsh employer, perhaps with their children at the same workplace. For some it must have seemed that this cycle would continue indefinitely as their children were forced to follow them into the trade.

There was little escape from that trade in 'Worstedopolis', as Bradford became known. The physical evidence could be seen in the hundreds of mill chimneys across the skyline, smoke and pollution belched out six days a week. Newspapers carried textile news and job adverts, and the trade was even part of the local dialect, with sayings such as 'chasing the sixpence' and 'trouble at t'mill'.

The mill as part of everyday life

Unlike across the Pennines in Lancashire, the West Yorkshire mills focused on worsted fabrics (yarn spun from wool fibres) rather than cotton. Bradford became famous for the quality of its worsted, and it was these mills that employed thousands of men and women over the years.

To put this dominance into context, on the 1851 census for the town, around 40 per cent of head of households (usually a male, sometimes a widow) were employed in the textile trade, but over the coming thirty years this would drop to 25 per cent. Children were also employed in the business, but this practice would decrease over time. By the 1851 census, only 5 per cent of under 8s in Bradford were working and by 1881 just half a per cent. Children over the age of 14, on the other hand, were expected to contribute towards the family income and regarded as adults by this age, certainly in working-class families. In 1851, 92 per cent of those aged 14 to 19 worked, and 82 per cent of these lived with the family and were therefore contributing to the household coffers.

Similarly, in a 1908-13 Board of Trade report, 71.5 per cent of single women in Bradford worked. A similar report of 1905 found that 26.6 per cent of boys and 23.1 per cent of girls worked either half-time or part-time, largely in the textile trade.

Before the Second World War, many working-class children were destined to enter the mill, just as their parents and grandparents had done before them as in other mill towns. In coal mining towns, such as Doncaster and Sheffield further south in the county, the predominant industry was where many children ended up.

The mill was part of life for many children for as long as they could remember, with children being sent into the mill on errands, or perhaps delivering lunch to a mother or father who worked there. When the time came to enter the mill on leaving school, jobs were often found by word of mouth and recommendation, rather than via a formal interview. Of course, mills did sometimes advertise in local papers, which also carried information on trading at the Wool Exchange, prices of wool and news and gossip from the industry.

An advert in the *Lancashire Evening Post* of 23 July 1901 stated that men or widows with families of workers were wanted for a Bradford worsted mill, with 'good wages and regular employment' offered to successful applicants. Textile dyeing was a spin-off of the textile trade, meaning that the whole textile production could be done within the city.

Women entering the mill came into a segregated workplace, with certain jobs done exclusively by either men or women. After the war, office work and the newly-established NHS brought about a wider variety of jobs which, coupled with competition from overseas textile production and a new wave of immigrants from Asia, meant that many who had seen families work in the mill for decades and even generations now left forever.

Wage disparities

The gulf between the wages and opportunities offered to men and women within the textile trade was wide. In Bradford, the trade was dominated by females in terms of numbers. However, women tended to do spinning and weaving while men were in wool sorting, which was better paid.

A Board of Trade report for 1908-13 found that a male wool sorter earned, on average, 32 shillings a week, whereas as a woman working two looms (a hard and physical job) would get no more than 17 shillings per week – the latter was not enough money to keep a family, yet many women had little choice but to try to get by on this if there was no male head of household – another reason teenagers were forced into the workplace to help keep family finances afloat.

The *Yorkshire Post* of March 1940 reported that 650 boys and girls were due to leave school, with a large proportion of them going to work in the mills of Bradford. Mr W. Pollack, manager of the Juvenile Employment Bureau, said around forty per cent of workers went into the mills, mainly induced by the wages. A boy of 16 doing dyeing and finishing would get 30s 1d per week, whereas a girl spinner of 18 would get 27s 7d. As late as 1946, male wool-combers were getting a minimum of 78s 1d for a daytime shift, whereas a woman took home 55s per week.

Even those with the security of a job in textiles were vulnerable to the stoppages that were very much a part of life. The *Leeds Mercury* of 30 October 1926 reported that James Drummond & Sons Ltd, worsted spinners and manufacturers, were to work short-time, employing between 600 and 700 workers for just three days a week instead of five. The decision had been made because of the 'coal stoppage'. A fortnight earlier, Salts Mill had also knocked its working week down to four days. Obviously, the loss of a portion of a family's income could hit the family finances hard, particularly where there was little spare for anything but the necessities at the best of times.

Despite the disparity of wages between the sexes, in the textile trade women were part of a relatively well-paid industry, but often returned home to roles where tradition was still enforced, particularly in immigrant communities keen to keep their culture and traditions alive.

Textile mill owners preferred women workers as they could pay them less and they believed that women employees were less likely to be involved in strikes. Perhaps for women the reality of balancing the family budget or paying the rent on their dwelling as a single person made them more reluctant to be involved in any political activity. Also, since meetings preceding a strike often took place in an evening, women with dependent children would simply not have been able to attend easily.

It would be impossible to describe what life was like for women in each of the city's textile mills and so in this chapter only Manningham Mills and Salt's Mill are covered in depth. Both employed thousands of women over the years and each played a key role within the community within which it stood.

Manningham Mills

Even well into the twenty-first century, Manningham Mills still dominates the Bradford skyline and is part of local folklore. The author can remember her grandmother telling her the popular Bradford legend that the top of the chimney was wide enough for a horse and carriage to be ridden around. Perhaps this was a distorted version of a story printed in the *Bradford Observer* of 19 November 1873, which reported that Lister and a group of his men partook of lunch at the top of the chimney shaft on the day after it was completed.

This imposing mill was created in 1871 by Samuel Lister and was known locally as Lister's Mill. In its Victorian heyday, it was the largest silk factory in the world and employed some 11,000 workers.

Before the first Manningham Mill (often known as Lilycroft Mill) was built, in 1838-39, there was a strong tradition of handloom weaving in the area. Bradford Local Studies Library volunteer Derek Barker has found evidence of around 200 such workers. Wool-combing was the last of the worsted processes to be mechanised.

Although this work was poorly paid, in comparison to the mill-work of later years, it could be carried out at a time dictated by the family rather than the employers. For example, breaks could be taken as and when needed, and if one member of the family was ill, the others could continue the work without a loss of pay.

The shift to factory-based textile work came at a cost, with the Luddite rebellions against machinery being moved into mills, taking the place of workers, both at home and in the mill. A sixty-hour working week was normal, with children working alongside adults as half-timers.

Finding information on female textile workers, and indeed any textile workers who were not management, is a challenge, as 'ordinary' individuals are rarely mentioned in official documents. Derek Barker writes:

> I have read thousands of Manningham Mills business letters. Not one is to a woman with the exception of very few to Lister's female relatives enquiring about cloth.

Yet female textile workers could, and did, have an influence on politics, as the Tillett Petition of 1892 proves. This document, which amounted to over a thousand signatures, was written to try to persuade trade union leader Ben Tillett to run for office as an Independent Labour candidate in Bradford. Tillett had asked for 1,000 signatures or more before he would agree to put himself forward for office. The document has been analysed by historians for the light that it sheds on both signatories and non-signatories, providing a window into mill-life at the end of the nineteenth century in the Manningham district.

Elizabeth Hardisty of Patent Street was one worker to be mentioned. On the petition she is described as a 53-year-old widow, living with her daughter Mary and working as a picker. She appears to have been something of a strong character. William Watson, the spinning manager at Manningham, said during the strike negotiations:

> It is quite true that her husband was killed here [at Manningham Mills]. She was then promised work in No. 3 warehouse and had it until the strike. At that time she was one of the chief leaders in causing the silk openers to go out. After a time a few returned to work and more promised but she intercepted them in Patent Street and prevented them from doing so. She has one daughter and no other means of livelihood but we understand that she has also a daughter that was a weaver ...

Another Manningham character was Martha Bradley, who was born in 1833 in the village of Addingham, sixteen miles from

Bradford, where the Listers had family connections. At the time of the Tillett Petition, Martha was 59 and living in Patent Street, the same road as Elizabeth Hardisty.

One might have expected Martha to be loyal to the Listers as her father had worked for the family, and in 1906, her obituary claimed she had performed sixty-two years of service – as she was in her mid-80s when she died, she must have begun working for the Listers in her mid-teens. She died within a few weeks of Samuel Lister and both are buried in Addingham.

Some indication of Martha's feisty character can be found in a letter from William Watson, who wrote to Lister in 1901:

> Last year you instructed me to give Old Martha a sovereign and when we gave her my Xmas box we thought she looked disappointed, so we have taken the liberty of giving her a sovereign from your Lordship and wished her on your behalf a Merry Xmas and Happy New Year feeling quite sure that you will approve of my action.

The Bradford mill women were renowned for their forthright character. Playwright J.B. Priestley remembered in his youth, in the early 1900s, a group of mill girls leaving work for the day could be quite a force to be reckoned with:

> I would find myself breasting a tide of shawls and something about my innocent dandyism would set them screaming at me and what I heard then, though I was never a prudish lad, made my cheeks burn.

Manningham Mills was known for its active leisure and welfare departments, which offered everything from an operatic society to sports days and charabanc trips. The mill had its own fields adjacent to the complex and, here, men and women would practice and compete in cricket, football, hockey, tennis and athletics, or join the gymnastics or swimming clubs.

The Manningham Mills strike

One of the most notable episodes in the history of Manningham Mill was the strike of 1890-91, which led directly to the forming of the Independent Labour Party. The strike was unusual in that women played a prominent role. Events began when a paper was pinned to a staff noticeboard in the mill announcing a change in wage rates. It would lead to a standoff that would draw in a whole community, attract the attention of an entire nation, and lead to the founding of a national political party.

The notice was posted on the board on an otherwise ordinary day on the run up to Christmas 1890 and, as soon as it was spotted, anger broke out. This was a particularly unfortunate time for Lister's to announce a reduction in wages for weavers, spinners and winders (a total of 1,100 workers), which the workers were told would come into effect on Christmas Eve.

A strike began that no one could have foreseen would last nineteen long weeks, through the bitterly cold winter months. This was a difficult time in the streets of Manningham, with families scratching a living and relying on charity to get by, while anyone who dared to speak out against the strikers or, even more audaciously, turn in to work at the mill, could expect verbal abuse and even physical violence.

For four and a half months the streets, which usually rang with the sound of clogged workers, had a different sound – desperation. A regular Thursday parade for women was organised, and they also took their children collecting door-to-door, not just in Bradford, but encouraging people in other towns to put their hands in their pockets in support of the strikers.

There must have been much bitterness amongst the striking workers, and even the general public, that Samuel Lister continued to enjoy a luxury lifestyle while his former employees had nothing. Women took part in protests against the wage cuts outside the town hall, the traditional place for voicing displeasure, while soup kitchens were set up to feed hungry families. Things reached such a pitch that troops were even dispatched to keep the peace.

At the height of the strike in January 1891, two female mill-hands were attacked and thrown down a flight of stone stairs for attempting to work during the strike. The women may have felt they had no choice but to try to bring money into their household, but fell foul of the strong feelings of the strikers and their families.

The strike committee was made up of sixteen women and eleven men. Among them were Mary Belton, Margaret A. Gott, Kate Sunderland, Georgina Sunderland, Harriet Catteral, Julia Ward, Mrs Pickles and Mrs Stevenson.

Finally, after a long and cold winter, the workers admitted defeat and returned to the mill in April 1891. They did so under humiliating conditions as their demands had not been met and they were now working for less pay.

Saltaire and the textile trade

No story of textiles in Bradford would be complete without exploring the role of the World Heritage village of Saltaire, founded by industrialist Titus Salt in 1851. Titus Salt came to Bradford with his parents in 1822 and, for almost thirty years, ran textile mills in the centre of Victorian Bradford, a town of great poverty and with a huge gap between rich and poor.

Whether or not Salt's reasons for creating a model village for his employees were wholly altruistic or had some aspect of either paternalism or self-interest, the move to Saltaire began a whole new chapter in the history of textiles. The opening ceremony for Salts Mill was one of the most opulent and well-attended parties that the town has ever known – and it encompassed lavish celebrations for Salt's 50th birthday and the 21st birthday of his son, Titus junior.

This special day took place on 20 September 1853, and it happened at a time before the other facilities of Saltaire were complete. Still to come were the housing for workers, leisure facilities, parkland and church.

At the opening ceremony, a banquet was held in the building's 'elaborately decorated' combing shed, whose fifty cast iron columns were wreathed with laurels, which must have made for a festive sight. There was a table for Salt and his principal guests, seven tables for unspecified 'ladies and gentlemen' and then twenty tables for the 2,440 guests who'd come in from Bradford on the train, as workers were not yet living in the village. How did they feel knowing they'd soon be working there? Perhaps excitement combined with a fear of the unknown, the feeling of having escaped the overcrowding and pollution coupled with the fear of starting again away from family and friends.

The huge opening ceremony feast comprised an incredible 120 legs of mutton, 100 dishes of lamb, 40 hams, 40 tongues, 50 pigeon pies, 50 dishes of roast chicken, 30 brace of grouse, 30 brace of partridge and 320 plum puddings, with 100 jellies and 100 dishes of tartlets. Such a spread must have made an impressive sight and the smells coming from the kitchen would have been like a hundred Sunday roasts all at once.

This tasty and filling fare was accompanied by grapes, melons and nectarines – exotic treats for the time that many people might not have tried before that day. Salt told the party he hoped he'd got the workers away from 'polluted air and water' and they would be a 'well fed, contented and happy body of operatives'. Once the feasting and speeches were over, the 2,000 guests returned to Bradford for a concert at St George's Hall, which itself had opened just a month before. As 'ordinary' workers crowded into the stalls for the concert, there must have been a real sense that Bradford was changing and perhaps at last for the better.

With the party over, the work in Saltaire would begin in earnest as workers started to enter the village and make a home there. Compared with life in central Bradford, a woman running a house in Saltaire, once the village and its amenities were all in place, must have seen many advantages. Chores such as drying washing and going to local shops or for a walk around the neighbourhood must have been much more pleasant without the fumes choked out by hundreds of mill chimneys. Most amenities, such as a bathhouse and the washhouses with running water, were contained within the village. And there were plenty of leisure facilities including a park, library, concert hall, gymnasium and a reading room. The houses themselves were of a better quality than the hastily-erected back-to-backs or converted old buildings that characterised working-class housing in inner Bradford.

But for most women, life may not have changed so much once the novelty of the new location had worn off. After all, bills still had to be paid and, despite creating the village and leisure facilities, Salt expected much from his workers and the hours at the mill could be long.

Single female mill-workers would perhaps have had more scope to take advantage of the social amenities on offer, including evening classes, lectures and sports clubs. Single people were offered housing in the three-storey buildings that interspersed some of the terraced workers' housing. Other accommodation was available above some of the shops. For younger women, school-age girls attended school on half-time alongside their mill employment and, in their leisure time, they could enjoy the park and river and cleaner, less polluted streets for their games and sports.

The families of the professional class of Saltaire workers were allocated bigger houses within the village, such as those that can still be seen on Shirley Street and Constance Street. Finally, the families of mill directors, if they chose to live in Saltaire rather than commute from more rural areas, would have lived in one of the twenty-two properties on Albert Road, Saltaire's most sumptuous street. Families of mill supervisors, ministers and teachers would have been able to afford this larger accommodation, with its extra living space.

Titus seems to have been well-liked by his workers at Saltaire – through the parties, parades and presentations and speeches that they arranged or attended. But this wasn't some kind of rural idyll. Salt would never bargain with strikers in his mills and insisted they came back to work before any kind of dialogue could take place, as newspaper reports that followed strikes and unrest attest.

Despite the attractive houses he provided for different grades of workers, Salt didn't actually live in the village. His house was seven miles south of Bradford, near Lightcliffe. On two occasions, thousands of his workers were invited there for parties, where they saw the beautiful house with alpacas roaming the lawns. Three thousand guests attended his 50th birthday and another 5,000 reportedly came along for his 70th, this time travelling to nearby Lightcliffe Railway Station, which had recently been built.

Although Salt's wife Caroline was present at the opening ceremony and party at the mill, in general the female members of the family had little to do with the village and its workers. Caroline Crossley married Titus on 21 August 1830 and the pair initially lived on North Parade. She was one of fourteen children and two of the pair's daughters (Lucy and Amelia) went on to marry wool men.

Salt's daughters were educated at home by a governess, as were the daughters of other textile barons. Four of his children were born at Crow Nest (Whitlam, Mary, Helen and Ada), two of whom died young.

The Newlands Mill Disaster

One of Bradford's worst and most shocking disasters was the collapse of a chimney at Newlands Mill. Fifty-four people were killed when the mill chimney fell after a stormy night on 28 December 1882. The youngest was Susan Woodhead, aged 8, and she was one of thirty-two children under the age of 18 killed on that day. Sixteen women were among the adult casualties.

There were more than 2,000 workers at Newlands, which was part of the Ripley Mill complex in West Bowling. In the mill on the morning of that fatal day, the talk would have been of Christmas – the presents received, the food eaten, and of what the coming year, 1883, would bring. How could any of the workers have imagined what would take place that morning?

It was only the second day back at work after the festive break and it would still have been dark when the workers arrived for their early shift, and only just beginning to get light at the time of the collapse. Although the death toll was high, the early time of day was actually a mercy in some respects, as many of the early shift workers had gone home for breakfast and to get their children ready for the day ahead.

As the debris was cleared and the scale of the accident became apparent, it took several days before some of the dead were recovered, which must have been an agonising wait for relatives. There was a terrible mistake when the funeral of Margaret Firth was about to take place after her body had supposedly been identified, when it was found to be a Margaret Ann Travis instead.

The local community rallied round and paid into a fund for those who'd lost family members. There was an attempt to bring a compensation claim to the assizes, but the jury were undecided on liability and so this failed. A total of £2,500 was collected locally and distributed, with a committee including the mayor and the president of the Chamber of Commerce deciding what was due. The only small compensation from the enquiry was that regret was expressed that the works hadn't been closed during repairs.

A memorial to those killed in the disaster stands at the corner of St Stephen's Road and Gaythorne Road in West Bowling and, in 2002, relatives of those killed gathered to unveil a new memorial stone at the site.

CHAPTER EIGHT

Migration

❖

For centuries, Bradford's history has been entwined with that of the many different individuals and communities who have made their home in the city, either from elsewhere in the UK or further afield. People have moved to Bradford temporarily for work during times of boom, settled here escaping from war, unrest or poverty in their home country, and been attracted to the area over the years due to stories of the plentiful work to be found, particularly in the textile trade.

Every immigrant will have had their own story, but there are many patterns and tales. An overriding theme of these stories is the positive impact immigrants have made to life in Bradford, and to the story of the city as a whole.

It's important not to look at immigration through rose-tinted glasses, as the stories here will show. Times of significant immigration can put a strain on both those entering a city, and those who already live and work there. Many of Bradford's newcomers have been forced to live in the worst accommodation, take jobs no one else was willing to carry out, and to bear the brunt of racism and prejudice.

And, of course, immigration is only half the story. Many thousands of people left Bradford to begin a new life elsewhere – largely for the same reasons that people came to the area: in search of a better life, because of the prospect of work, or to join friends and family already in the city. Bradford's industries have been affected by hard times as well as boom times, and a slump in trade often caused large numbers of people to leave Bradford for elsewhere in the UK, or even a different country.

IMMIGRATION

Germany

Perhaps the most high-profile group of immigrants for the period 1850 to 1950 are those who came to Bradford from Germany, eventually establishing the district that is now one of the city's finest heritage attractions, and home to several listed buildings.

Bradford's German immigrants had already been settled in the town for a generation. Arriving in the 1820s and 1830s, these incomers came to the town in response to Bradford's growing dominance of the textile trade. While the town's businessmen had the knowledge and means to produce worsteds, most textile merchants lacked the know-how for exporting their goods in large volume. And this is where the new arrivals had a gap to fill.

The German textile businesses became established in what would become known as 'Little Germany', close to Bradford Cathedral, where the community built warehouses for the export of goods. Although there were never more than around 1,000 Germans living in Bradford at any one time, the newcomers played their part in the commercial, political and charitable aspects of life in the town. Many of these merchants and their families were German Jews, and it was largely for their benefit and through their efforts that Bowland Street synagogue opened in 1881.

Another notable group of German immigrants was the pork butchers, who arrived in the mid-nineteenth century serving pies, pork sausages and pigs' trotters to the shoppers of Bradford. These were family-run businesses who worked long hours, with both husband and wife involved in the retail outlet. These butchers were part of a UK-wide immigration wave, entrepreneurs keen to take advantage of the population boom brought about by the Industrial Revolution in Britain. Most of these tradesmen and their families came from the southern region of Hohenlohe, where an agricultural depression had forced people off the land.

Until the outbreak of the First World War, German immigrants seem to have been accepted into the city. Many of the Hohenlohe butchers felt so settled that they sent letters home asking the young women of their village to join them to form a family unit, while other German-based families sent their young men to learn the trade from emigrant Germans already settled in the UK, suggesting a settled immigrant community.

The first few weeks of the First World War proved that life in the UK would not be easy for resident Germans from then on. Very quickly, those Bradford women who married German men were forced to register as enemy aliens, as were their children, something that must have been a shock for a woman who might have grown up in Bradford, only to find herself branded an outlaw in her own home city.

Many families faced the stark choice of being separated from their German male breadwinner or leaving the country. Those families who chose to remain had to register at their local police station and have their movements monitored, as well as facing potential hostility from neighbours and work colleagues. Although the *Bradford Daily Telegraph* of 20 August 1914 said that the Germans and their families who remained 'may be regarded as friendly', they were actually banned from using telephones or motor cars and their movements were subject to scrutiny in a sad foreshadowing of the hostilities that would mark the coming years.

Ireland

In contrast to the integration of the German immigrants to Bradford, at least until the outbreak of war with Germany, were the experiences of Irish immigrants. Thousands arrived in Bradford in the 1840s as part of a large wave of immigration from Ireland to the UK, caused by the potato famine, which decimated many rural Irish communities between the years 1845 and 1852. More than a million people left Ireland during this terrible time – between a fifth and a quarter of the island's population.

Within ten years of the start of the Irish arriving, around a tenth of Bradford's population was Irish. As tends to be the pattern with large-scale arrivals in any town, the immigrants were forced initially to inhabit the poorest areas, in this case the Broomfields area and the streets around St Mary's Church (the original building of 1825, later rebuilt) on the East Parade/ Barkerend Road junction.

Most immigrants would gravitate to a certain area, often where their fellow countrymen were living, both for moral and physical support, and because of proximity to any available places of work. Over the years, the area would begin to gain something of the overriding characteristics of its immigrant population, with shops, places of worship and leisure facilities most often arranged by the community themselves and patronised and staffed largely by people from that group of incomers.

The majority of Irish newcomers came from Mayo and Sligo, both largely rural districts in Ireland's west. Families who had been making a living from the land now arrived in a town with more than 100,000 inhabitants that was already very much in the grip of the Industrial Revolution. Few spoke English as their first language and the welcome they received wasn't always warm.

Life could be hard for families who'd left largely rural farming communities to arrive in this Victorian town, which already had some of the worst poverty in the UK. Around three-quarters of the new arrivals couldn't read or write English. Nelson Court and Bedford Street were centres for Irish immigrants, with many living in slums and perhaps even taking in lodgers to help with the rent. By the start of our period, St Mary's Church had already been established for twenty-five years. Father John Motler created churches at St Joseph's and St Peter's. Religion would have been a big consolation for immigrant women, giving them focus and companionship as well as the opportunity to socialise and help others in similar situations.

Many of Bradford's Catholic families are descended from these immigrants of the 1850s and earlier. By 1851, Bradford had 9,581 Irish people in a population of 103,000. The first of the immigrant women, if they worked, were forced to enter unskilled or manual labour jobs. More than eighty per cent of the hawkers and pedlars in the city during the 1850s were Irish.

Jewish immigration

The high profile and large Jewish population of nearby Leeds has overshadowed the story of Bradford's Jewish community and its role in the life of the city but, nevertheless, the story of the immigration of Jews to Bradford has an interesting and distinct character.

Bradford's first synagogue was a non-orthodox place of worship that opened in 1881 on Bowland Street, off Manningham Lane. This was a prosperous area, close to Victorian villas and private roads created for wealthy industrialists, their families and servants. Nearby Mount Royd Villas, still a private road, is a perfect example of the type of streets once inhabited by 'merchant princes', keen to have privacy yet remain close to the city and their place of business. This street of imposing three- and four-storey homes looked onto tennis courts and woodland, just a few hundred yards from the shops and businesses of Manningham Lane yet was almost a rural idyll. Humbert Wolfe, an Italian-born author of Jewish descent, lived on this street.

One of the most high-profile Jewish couples was Florence and Jacob Moser, a philanthropic pair who gave thousands of pounds to charitable causes during their time in the city. Another prominent incomer was Olive Messer, born in Leeds in 1928 to Dolly and Sidney Dawson, who both worked in retail. Olive moved to the city with her GP husband Dr Basil Messer in 1948 and she was a conservative councillor in Shipley in 1957 becoming lord mayor in 1984 which, although after our period, shows that women who'd been in the city during that time did go on to public office. Olive died in 2011 and there's a memorial to her in Lister Park.

Ella Matilde Henriette Luker (1880-1978)

A Denmark-born lady active in Bradford during the 1930s, Ella opened an unemployment centre for women during the Great Depression, which saw families all over the country struggle. She was of the earliest women graduates in the whole world (she studied at London University) and moved to Bradford when her husband Herbert's work as a director of a manufacturing firm brought them to the city.

Ella's unemployment centre taught its patrons knitting and Esperanto – a constructed 'second' language popular at the time that was intended to give people a second language with which to communicate. When the Prince of Wales visited the centre during his tour of Yorkshire in 1933, he was greeted in this language.

The end of our period comes just before the start of one of the largest waves of immigration into Bradford, the large-scale movement of people from Asia and Africa, who entered the city in the years following the Second World War.

EMIGRATION

Although much of the flow has been into the city rather than out of it, there have, of course, been many emigrations over the decades. Families have left during times of downturn in their trade, or on hearing of new opportunities in other towns or even other countries – some have returned and others have made their home elsewhere.

The *Morning Post* of 7 March 1857 reported on the progress of a party of Bradford families who were invited to Moreton Bay in Australia, having 'picked families from the wool-combers in this district'. Letters home, said the newspaper, spoke in a 'cheerful and satisfactory strain' of conditions in their new country and they 'earnestly recommended as many more as possible' to follow them to their new home – perhaps hoping to set up a community of Bradfordians on the other side of the world.

In Australia, the Moreton Bay newspaper said that, because there was a labour shortage there and the 'depressed state of a considerable number of families', their emigration commission decided to invite people over. Applicants had to be under the age of 40 and willing to work in one of a number of trades, including female domestic servant, agricultural labourer, mason or blacksmith. Those successful would receive a free passage to Australia.

Similarly, in 1879, a group of engineers and machinists left Bradford for America by train, via Liverpool. The emigrants included the chairman of the Bradford strike committee (the men leaving had been apparently on strike for some time), and another group was due to leave the following week. The next year, a group of fifty female textile operatives left for Philadelphia, where an 'eminent manufacturing firm' had already offered them jobs.

Around this time, the National Steamship Company had an office in Westgate, from which people could arrange a passage overseas, whether for business, pleasure or emigration. Steamers regularly went to New York, Boston, Philadelphia and Baltimore for £6, carrying passengers from the National Steamship Company.

In the years following the textile depression, which had seen a strike at Lister's Mill, for many it seemed as if the best opportunities were to be found overseas. The more textile workers who moved over to the US, the more confident this made prospective emigrants, as they heard back news from friends and relatives who had made the break and knew there would be friendly faces waiting to meet them in their new home. The town of Boston in Massachusetts was talked of as being the 'Bradford of America', with Bradford-trained male and female textile workers exporting their skills out of the city and taking employment at the Bradford-originated firm of Messrs Willey & Co at South Barne in the US.

Finally, in 1912, a group of millworkers was detained in Boston, US, for a breach of immigration laws. Apparently, an unscrupulous agent had taken advantage of the mill men and women's eagerness to leave the country and was to go on trial for inducing contract labourers to go to America. At this stage, around a dozen workers were leaving the city every week, some going to the Bradford firms set up in Boston.

CHAPTER NINE

Women in Wartime: Bradford in the Two World Wars

❖

The two world wars brought great change, of both a temporary and a permanent nature. In each of these global conflicts, the city's women stepped forward to take the place of men in the workplace, to man the Home Front and to volunteer to help those affected by war, as well as continue to look after the home and family.

Bradford women in the First World War

The story of the outbreak of the First World War is all too familiar to many of us, with the assassination of Archduke Franz Ferdinand of Austria and his wife Sophie, Duchess of Hohenberg, on 28 June 1914, setting into motion a chain of events that would see more than 70 million personnel mobilised in a five-year conflict that killed more than 16 million people.

The effect of the war came to Bradford quickly, as it did to many UK cities, although we can now understand with hindsight that most people initially underestimated the scale and length of the conflict. Within a day of war being declared, public train journeys into and out of Bradford and other cities were already being cancelled as trains were mobilised for troops. The Bradford Territorials (1/6th West Yorkshire Regiment) were the first in England to declare themselves 'ready to move', having mobilised on 4 August, arriving in France after training on 15 April 1915.

As the mobilising troops left Bradford Exchange Station, waved off by tearful wives, mothers and other family members, ironically with them went a group of around fifty German men who were reserves for their home country – just a few short weeks earlier they had been part of the fabric of Bradford's commercial and social life and now they were travelling 'home' and might well face their former comrades on the battlefield before long. It mattered little that, by this point, so well regarded and settled was Bradford's German community that two Germans had been mayor: Jacob Moser and Charles Semon. Germany was now the enemy and people were told to be on their guard against foreign spies.

The earliest signs that the city was at war were apparent within days of the outbreak of hostilities, when Lister Park closed to the public on 6 August and armed guards were visible, as guns, supplies and ammunition began to arrive for the Army Service Corps. What might have seemed an exciting sight to the young children of the surrounding streets, as they watched the soldiers preparing to leave for the Front, must have put fear into the hearts of those old enough to understand what this meant, particularly those who had lived through conflicts such as the Boer War.

The reality of war

Within the first weeks of the First World War, the Bradford Guild of Help saw its appeals for help rise tenfold as men left behind families who were soon in need of aid. Once the breadwinner had left the family home, a soldier's pay didn't go far and it wasn't always possible for women to find a job that would fit in around caring for the family.

Even when army pay was promised, it could be slow in arriving and, in some cases, children were given temporary tickets to get free school meals while their appeal for aid was processed. Further financial difficulties affected even those who hadn't yet enlisted, as short-term working measures were put into place in various organisations, leaving families short of their usual income.

The wives and mothers of those who had enlisted had to fill in forms to claim money and were instructed to apply to the city hall for assistance. It's easy to imagine the anxious conversations about the progress of the war and the snippets of news that took place as people queued to make their application. How long would it be before the Germans were beaten and the soldiers could return home? Would the men be home before Christmas?

The first festive season of the war must have been an anxious time for many families, who tried to make the best of the celebrations, all the time coming to the realisation that the war would not soon be over as many had hoped. The year 1915 brought a fresh appeal for recruits, and an illuminated tramcar toured the city's main streets each evening, encouraging men to do their bit for king and country and sign-up for the forces. Its appearance made a stark contrast to the darkness of winter nights and the mental gloom that set in as it became clear that the war would be long and costly.

Jessie Millar Wilson – the much-loved 'Auntie J'

Bradford-born Jessie Millar Wilson MBE was the daughter of a wool merchant who took up the suffragette cause. However, at the outbreak of the First World War, when she was aged 43, she decided to put votes for women to one side, leave her job as a gardener and sign-up as a Young Men's Christian Association (YMCA) volunteer on the Front after hearing of the terrible conditions in the trenches and the number of casualties.

Out at the Western Front, Jessie joined thousands of other YMCA volunteers who provided that most simple but most appreciated of comforts – a canteen. From here she helped dispense tea, cake and friendly chat to the soldiers, even helping individual soldiers to compose letters home.

So well-loved was Jessie that she became known to the troops as Auntie J, and many of the men kept in touch with her for years after the war. She stayed overseas until 1921, later receiving an MBE (Member of the British Empire) for her work.

Once the initial flurry of recruitment and jingoism had died down, newspaper reports from the Front brought daily gloom, with poignant photographs and reports of men killed in action. As 1914's Bradford Sanitary Association annual report remarked:

Long working hours, restricted opportunities for recreation and relaxation, our darkened streets, the increased cost of living and the rigid economy which must be practised tend to lower the vital energy of all.

Although rationing wasn't introduced until 1917, early on there were shortages of food and clothes as the realities of supplying the troops overseas meant that goods were diverted elsewhere and people were expected to 'make do and mend'.

WARTIME WORK FOR WOMEN

As men left for the Front and many returned home badly maimed, it soon became clear that the war would be a protracted one and that the need to recruit female workers would be a priority. These new conditions brought about opportunities for women in both the paid and voluntary sectors.

From December 1915, the Bradford War Hospital (now St Luke's Hospital) offered beds to soldiers, through and beyond the end of war, until July 1919. Opportunities for nurses, auxiliaries and volunteers, such as ward visitors, opened up, particularly with auxiliary hospitals around the city in locations including Clayton, Bowling Park and Saltaire. By the end of the war the city could make around 2,500 hospital beds available, with even schools providing accommodation for the wounded.

Matron Mitchell of Saltaire

Hannah Mitchell, matron of Sir Titus Salt Hospital in the First World War, was a well-known and liked figure of authority who ran her hospital as a tight ship. She trained at Bradford Royal Infirmary and, at the outbreak of war, had already been matron at Salt's hospital for more than fifteen years. The first wartime patients arrived on 6 May 1915 in a group of ten – four of whom had bayonet or shrapnel wounds. They would be the first of many soldiers the people of the village of Saltaire would take to their hearts, donating biscuits, tobacco, eggs and jam, with men too old for active service volunteering their time to take those patients well enough out on trips.

Schools in the First World War

During the early months of the First World War, the initial fervour of the recruitment campaign, which sent thousands of Bradford men to the Front, left many families back home in difficulties. Teachers reported children coming into school hungry and having to be provided with breakfast, lunch and even tea. In 1915, Margaret McMillan, seeing first-hand the effect of the war on those who remained at home, recommended that primary schools provide beds for younger children to rest as many were exhausted through hunger and poverty.

Despite the hardship many families faced, children were encouraged to play their part in the war effort by collecting goods to sell to raise money, or holding events such as jumble sales. As the months went by, rolls of honour saluting the fallen were read out in school assemblies, which must have been distressing for children, such as when the Bradford Pals were slain in 1916 and the city lost 1,700 men over the course of several days on the Somme, with many more returning home with life-changing physical and mental injuries.

Louisa Pesel and the Khaki Club

Louisa Pesel (1870-1947) was a Bradford-born embroidery teacher who, during the First World War, put her talent for handicrafts to lasting use by setting up the Khaki Club. This work was quite different to her time spent in the West Riding branch of the Needlework Guild. In the Khaki Club at Forster Square, this daughter of a German merchant helped injured soldiers returning from the war find rehabilitation through the power of needlework. Shell-shocked soldiers were tasked with the seemingly incongruous work of learning to embroider and, through absorption in the craft, were able to temporarily escape their pain and mental anguish.

The Khaki Club offered much more than handicrafts, though. It was also a place where injured soldiers could have a meal, choose a library book, enjoy a board game and even attend a concert.

Louisa wrote the book *Practical Canvas Embroidery*, which was one of several handbooks she authored. This one had different stitches and designs as well as a preface by A.J.B. Wace, keeper of the department of textiles at the Victoria and Albert Museum in London. She dedicated the book to Queen Mary, who had shown interest in her work. It was originally published in 1929 and is still available from vintage bookshops today.

Louisa's good worked continued in the Second World War, when she organised the assembly of embroidery kits to send out to British prisoners-of-war, which they used for therapy and as a challenge during the long months of imprisonment.

Working on a similar premise to the Khaki Club, The Shipley War Service Club helped the dependants of serving soldiers and sailors, providing a club-room where they could meet for 'recreation, instruction and sympathy'. It met twice a week at the premises of Shipley Co-operative Society and was part of a national programme of clubs organised by Lady Jellicoe and Lady French. Among the activities were cookery demonstrations, a lantern lecture on Baghdad and an evening of sewing competitions. There was also a savings bank and an annual flag day to raise funds.

Another option for women to do their bit for the war effort was by becoming involved in the manufacture of munitions. Several large workplaces converted to munitions as the war progressed, with Lister's Mill making shell silk linings, the National Shell Factory operating on the Valley Dyeworks site from November 1915, followed by the Phoenix Dynamo Munitions factory making shells in 1916.

Obviously, this type of work was physically hard and risky, as an explosion at Heckmondwike showed in the first winter of the war, followed by a serious explosion at Low Moor munitions where picric acid was produced. Despite the dangers, many women carried out heavy work in one of the area's eight munition factories, or in ironworks, dyeworks and even locomotive sheds, workplaces which, until the outbreak of war, had been the province of male workers.

Portrait-painter Flora Lion was tasked by the Ministry of Information with painting factory scenes in Bradford and Leeds, and she captured everyday scenes such as women queueing wearily for a meal and a cup of tea partway through their shift. One of her most famous works *is Women's Canteen at Phoenix Works, Bradford.*

Isabel Salt

Isabel Salt, the granddaughter of Sir Titus Salt, spoke out on women's work in wartime, stating that women should receive better pay for the responsible jobs they were carrying out. She also called for a Christian 'push' for the abolition of war, with the words: 'The only way to kill a wrong idea is by the spread of right ideas.'

The Low Moor explosion

The Low Moor explosion of 21 August 1916 killed thirty-eight and injured more than a hundred people, with the huge explosion being heard as far away as York, forty miles to the north east. It took fire-crews a full three days to extinguish the fire and the debris was found for miles around. The incident was not reported in newspapers because of wartime restrictions, but men, women and children were injured, and the incident even affected a wedding ceremony taking place nearby, when the bride was hit by flying glass.

Despite the efforts of Bradford's women, and women all around the country, to keep life running smoothly in the absence of the men, there were many complaints that women were unable to do the jobs that men could do. Or there was the question of whether, when the servicemen eventually returned, there would be jobs for them to come back to. For example, in November 1916, the *Leeds Mercury* announced some friction over the introduction of female wool-sorters in Bradford mills, with men asking for a guarantee of reinstatement on their return.

The issue of women driving trams during wartime was a hard-fought one, with the manager of Bradford Corporation Tramways grumbling about their employment in 1915, and complaints of women not being strong enough to operate the brakes on the trams. An article in the *Yorkshire Post* in January 1917 asked: 'Are lady conductors able to apply brakes?' after an accident in Wyke where 26-year-old Jeannie Kathleen Regan was killed when the Bradford Corporation tramcar on which she was working hit a motor car – a runaway vehicle with no driver. Twenty other people were injured and two would later die. At the inquest, Bradford Corporation accepted liability and admitted that 'a more practical tuition' of conductresses was needed.

The experiences of women working throughout the Great War, as well as the granting of the vote to women and the gradual emergence of women onto the political scene, meant that at the outbreak of the Second World War, the fact that women workers would be taking the place of men was a given.

Once again, the female population took its place filling vacancies left by servicemen, whether in the mills, on public transport, or even shop work. This time, there were many opportunities for women to volunteer from the outset. The 'Your Country Needs You' campaign called for women to enter the services. In January 1942, the *Yorkshire Post* reported that an appeal had been made for women to undertake part-time work and 174 women had applied, including 'many elderly women'. Work on offer was in factories and the new workers replaced other women who'd been called-up. The new recruits would benefit from arranging their working hours to fit in around any household duties, as many textile mills had also done during peacetime.

As early as 1937, two years before the outbreak of the Second World War, Bradford's police chief mused that there was no reason women should not offer their services as air-raid wardens and telephonists should war come again. Indeed, by 1939 one in ten air-raid wardens in the Bradford district was female. However, not all agreed with the new appointments. A few months after the start of the Second World War, the former chief constable of Bradford, Joseph Farndale, complained that 'slips of girls' would be of no use in an air-raid when acting as wardens. He believed that such roles should only be taken on by mature women who wouldn't 'take fright'.

EVERYDAY LIFE IN WARTIME

The city didn't suffer the heavy aerial bombardment of industrial centres such as Liverpool, Coventry and London, but in both wars, everyday life was strongly affected.

In each war, rationing and food shortages affected that most basic of household tasks – cooking – and, of course, shopping. Families were advised to 'make do and mend', to use up every scrap of food and to grow their own produce where possible, which of course was only possible for those with enough land, although even a small garden with flower beds could be dug over.

Isobel Grimshaw remembers her mother cooking 'bird's nests' which was a fried egg dropped onto a bed of mashed potato, and also corned beef hash or fritters.

Rationing was something that would have affected Bradford women greatly, whether or not they were responsible for feeding a family. In both wars, queues outside shops were a common sight as people waited eagerly when word got out that popular food stuff was in stock. Petrol and clothes rationing again meant changes – fewer cars out on leisure trips – and there was a keen demand for those who were good with a needle and could mend or alter garments.

Wherever there are ration regulations there are those who go against the rules, either on a small scale or as part of a larger concern. Prosecutions for going against ration regulations were common. In February 1940, Mrs Elizabeth Bates of Copley Street appeared in court for unlawfully obtaining 28oz of sugar and 36oz of bacon in excess of her ration. An official from the local food control committee had been in the shop at the time the offence occurred and the shopkeeper was also called to appear in court. They were called in as a warning, but three months' imprisonment or a £100 fine could be levied in some cases.

The metal fences of parks and public buildings were often requisitioned for the war effort, and even at street level in the Second World War, houses and backyards took on a new look as bomb shelters were dug or constructed in gardens and public places, and windows were blacked out in case of air-raids. As recently as 2014, an air-raid shelter sign was discovered in City Hall, which had once been used to direct members of the public to a shelter within the building.

Bradford Women's Humanity League

On 9 September 1917, a mass demonstration of 3,000 men and women took place, organised by the Bradford Women's Humanity League. Departing from the Textile Hall at Piece Hall Yard (where a plaque now commemorates the event), the huge procession moved through the city to Carlton Street, followed by a rally in the grounds of Textile School, calling for peace. This protest came after three years of unrelenting war and daily newspaper headlines of death, maiming and orphaned children – the call for peace would have struck a chord with many.

The league, which was founded just ten days after conscription was introduced and met weekly at Laycock's Café on Tyrrel Street, has left few records. However, there is written reference to the banners carried at the march, which included the slogans 'The boys in the trenches want peace' and 'I want my daddy'. Although the demonstration went off peaceably, the aims of the league were not looked upon kindly by all. One of the league's members, Fanny Muir of Frizinghall, found herself in court in May 1918, in what the *Leeds Mercury* called a case of 'slandering young soldiers'. According to the newspaper report, Fanny had spoken out against the war in Shipley market-place, telling the gathered crowd that she'd been told by a Scottish soldier about appalling conditions on the Front, grown men crying for their mothers, and boys aged between 15 and 18 fighting under-age. Officers of the Seaforth Highlanders and Royal Engineers denied Fanny's accusations and she was fined £50 under the Defence of the Realm Act.

Voluntary work and charity

The two world wars opened up the opportunity for women to work as volunteers for the war effort, both inside and outside the home. Opportunities ranged from small-scale solo enterprises, such as knitting socks for the troops, through to welcoming soldiers or refugees arriving in Bradford, visiting the wounded in hospital, or simply encouraging others to get involved in wartime fundraising.

For those injured and sent to a hospital in the Bradford district, it would often be the comforts provided by well-meaning local women that brought cheer and hope. Christmas 1916 was sombre and sobering, just months after the tragic Battle of the Somme, in which thousands of Bradford men lost their lives or were injured. Nurse Mitchell of Sir Titus Salt Hospital, having enlisted donations from Shipley and Saltaire communities, gave the injured men in her hospital a Christmas to remember with a huge roast turkey, which she carved herself at the head of the table, followed by a plum pudding, 'which entered in flaming glory, decked with holly'. Next came trifle and crackers, with music from the Salvation Army and Shipley Band. The daughters and nieces of local Councillor Rhodes came along to lend their voices to the sing-song, with popular tunes and carols at what must have been a jolly occasion amid the terrible gloom.

A year later, at a concert fundraiser, Nurse Mitchell noted that many of the Saltaire and Shipley villagers were reluctant to take money from the returning heroes:

> We Shipley people are honoured by having the wounded soldiers in our midst and we must see that they are well treated … I have also to return thanks for certain acts of violence towards the "boys" as when the barber ran after one of them with his razor when he offered to pay for a shave. The good shopkeepers who will not be paid for rubber tips for crutches and drapers who give them three handkerchiefs when they go to buy one.

Another option for women hoping to lend a hand during the Great War was volunteering with the Bradford's Lady Mayoress's War Guild, which took in garments for those in need, and distributed over 16,000 items within two months of the outbreak of war. The guild was a well-organised and well-thought-of charity which managed to cover the whole city and regularly held fundraising events in the form of 'flag days', where members of the public made a donation to a fund that sent 'personal comforts' to soldiers serving overseas. Young women were invited through newspaper appeals to become flag-day collectors, or to join the guild, which not only provided fighting men at home and abroad with clothes and underwear, but also treats for those invalided home to hospital, including hot meals, cigarettes and tobacco.

Members of the public were encouraged to drop off their parcels of donations at the town hall, and lists of contributors were regularly published in newspapers. All ages were involved. Schoolchildren sent presents of eggs and cakes via their schools, while church and youth group children took fruit to the hospitalised soldiers on Sundays, and the guild provided fresh flowers for the hospital each week. The group was certainly ahead of its time in trying to brighten up the environment of the wounded and give them things to look forward to, including visits from family, who were accommodated by guild volunteers if the need arose.

Working in a similar vein was Shipley Distress Committee, whose president was a Lady Denby. During the First World War its members worked on garments which were sent to various charities including the Red Cross Society, and Queen Mary's Needlework Guild. In fact, members received a letter from Queen Mary's lady in waiting who wrote to thank them for their donations. They also made garments for local recruits to take with them, including shirts, socks, belts and caps. The group worked at the Saltaire Institute for two hours an afternoon, twice a week.

MIGRATION DURING THE WORLD WARS

Bradford's history during two World Wars is entwined with immigration and emigration. Both provided a safe haven for those fleeing persecution, but there were sad episodes of the city turning against long-standing citizens simply because of their country of origin.

In the First World War, the city took in hundreds of Belgian refugees. Just seven years before the outbreak of war, sports fans had enjoyed watching the Belgian national water polo team at the Corporation Baths, where they had beaten the Bradford Dolphins after watching a diving display by divers of both nations – no one could have guessed that it would not be long before the nations were embroiled within a longstanding conflict. Not long after the outbreak of the Great War, a party of Belgian refugees arrived, after the city assured national authorities it could accommodate up to 600 refugees.

On the whole, Bradford provided a warm welcome to those new arrivals, so much so that people actually lined the streets to welcome the Belgians as they entered the city, and several relief funds were set up to help them. The *Leeds Mercury* of 16 October 1914 reported 'stirring scenes' as crowds of up to 100,000 turned out to see the new arrivals.

The city's Baths Hall had been kitted out as a reception centre, and women and children had their own quarters separate from the men, with cards in French and Flemish, informing them of the arrangements that had been set in place. Among those providing a welcome were three Catholic nuns from Leeds who had lived in Belgium. The well-dressed women and girls of the party were welcomed from their train by cheering crowds and the lord mayor, alongside religious representatives.

Some of the incomers were housed in Shipley, and the Shipley Distress Committee and Miss Mitchell, the matron of Saltaire Hospital, oversaw their care at Shipley Grange. There was a committee of ladies, including Lady Denby and a Mrs Schultan, and also a housing and furnishing committee. Shipley Distress Committee came to the aid of the incomers by issuing a call for toys for the children as well as the loan of items such as cooking utensils, rugs and bedding.

However, the intention was for the refugees to rely on charity as little as possible, since the Belgian king had announced that he wished his countrymen to take up jobs in their temporary home country. And so the newcomers were told to present themselves at the Labour Exchange as soon as possible. Nevertheless, inevitably there were calls that the incomers would be taking British jobs. Several hundred Belgians left to return to their home country in 1919.

The letters pages of newspapers often give an indication of different feelings about the various groups of immigrants, the things being done to help them, but sadly also the resentment that sometimes flared up. There are also job adverts that mention refugees seeking a position in service or as a labourer, usually for manual work, perhaps because of the language barrier.

In October 1914, a Mr Jan Hendricks wrote an open letter to the lord mayor, which was published in local newspapers, saying 'we are most grateful for the kindness and attention that has been extended to us'. The lord and lady mayoress had visited the refugees at the centre where they were staying to ensure they were well cared for.

Many immigrant parents encouraged their children to work hard and were ambitious for them, hoping they would aspire to more than the manual labour work that they themselves might have been forced to take to begin with.

During the two wars, Bradford was at times both a place of refuge and a place from which to escape – with refugees entering the city and evacuees leaving. In the Second World War, Bradford, as with many other cities, was one of the locations to welcome children in the *Kindertransport* scheme. Manningham had a hostel for Jewish children, many of whom ended up making their lives in the city on a permanent basis and whose descendants still live locally.

With the threat of air-raids and uncertainty about how much of an enemy target the city would be, around 500 Bradford children were evacuated to Nelson in Lancashire, as well as to the Yorkshire towns of Harrogate and Mirfield. As in many towns, these children were soon called back to their homes by parents as the 'phoney war' continued. A lord mayor's fund provided money to kit-out the evacuee children leaving Bradford with a coat and boots. One Lancashire lady wrote to the *Leeds Mercury* in October 1939 to say that children were being sent out to their new homes in a pitiable state, including two children with 'neither shoes nor clothing', who'd reportedly had no mother for the past five years. A party was given for the children who remained in Keighley at Christmas 1944, and they were visited by Bradford's lord mayor and assured him they were being well cared for.

In turn, as war progressed and bombing intensified around London and port cities such as Liverpool and Southampton, Bradford began to take its own evacuees, with almost 5,000 from London alone in 1944. Cooking depots supplied food and there were also rest centres and school shelters. The rest centres were used until people could be sent out to their permanent billets.

Thousands of women were coming and going during the Second World War. In December 1941, a contingent set out on a special train to volunteer at the Royal Ordnance Factory in Staffordshire. The elderly, middle-aged and young women were given a civic send-off – many had previously worked in textiles and had been signed up by women from the factory on a recruiting tour.

CHAPTER TEN

Leisure and Entertainment

❖

Bradford has long offered a lively social scene, and our period covers a number of exciting developments that happened at this time, including the coming of cinema, the establishment of societies and groups based around a particular hobby, a regular programme of special events, such as parades, fairs and pageants, as well as an increase in leisure time as workers began to demand, and receive, more from their employers.

Although many of the above are common to towns and cities the length and breadth of the UK, we'll be exploring what made leisure time in Bradford different to anywhere else, and what women enjoyed doing. To some extent, how leisure time was spent depended upon the amount of time and money available. But some of the finest entertainment on offer cost very little and appealed to women and men from a variety of backgrounds.

CLUBS AND SOCIETIES

The Victorian era was a golden age for clubs and societies, although many of these were aimed at men, at least initially. A growing postal system, the expansion of public transport and the availability of local newspapers all made it easier to organise club meetings and recruit new members, as well as to stay in touch with fellow members and organise activities such as visiting speakers, meals out, etc.

For many women, the local place of worship was a mainstay of their social life. Churches and chapels offered amateur dramatic societies (such as the Bradford Catholic Players), bible-reading, choirs and fundraising groups. Such societies could be of particular value to immigrant women where an immigrant community and a place of worship was already established, offering the chance to find their feet in a friendly environment.

Other groups were arranged around a particular hobby or interest, such as sewing, baking or reading, and the main political groups also had branches for women, or welcomed women to their meetings.

Literary activities

Bradford Subscription Library

Bradford Subscription Library has its origins in 1774, when Bradford was a town of around 4,000 inhabitants. This was the year John Wesley visited Bradford and the canal reached the town – communications were opening up.

From its earliest years the library seems to have had no bar against women office holders. In 1829, the librarian was a Miss Eliza Croft and then a Miss Mason, and Miss Rhodes followed, with the latter giving more than thirty years of service as assistant and full librarian, ending up with two female assistants herself.

The library's premises in Darley Street were opened in 1854. This thoroughfare was once part of a semi-rural manorial estate, but by the mid-1800s was a bustling shopping street with a good footfall. The earliest subscribers to the library seem to have been mainly men (including the Reverend Patrick Brontë, father of the Brontë sisters), as were the committee members, with just a few women named, including a Miss Bower as a subscriber.

Female authors of Bradford

Women authors of this period from Bradford have been fairly hard to track down. One of the best known is Dorothy Black, born in the city in 1890. She wrote more than a hundred romance novels and, like her fellow novelists the Brontës, sometimes went under a male pen-name, in this case Peter Delius (Delius was a family name and Dorothy was the niece of notable musician Frederick Delius).

Another literary notable was Elizabeth Southwart, the author and playwright who wrote *Thornton Moors & Villages*, which was published in 1923, and *The Passport to Fairyland*. Her novel *The Story of Jenny* was told through the eyes of a 12-year-old mill-girl who grew up to experience the loss of her lover in the war.

In her day, Elizabeth was perhaps best known for her drama rather than her books. Her play *Ishmael* was performed at the Leeds Civic Playhouse in 1930 and *The Third Generation*, a comedy in three acts, was performed at Colne Congregational Church in 1946. *Billy's Wife* was aired on North Regional Radio in 1931. *Ishmael* was also performed at The Strand Theatre in London, *The Stage* newspaper announced in May 1927. It was described as a 'West Yorkshire Farm Play'. However, the actors seemed to have struggled with the northern setting, since the Yorkshire dialect was 'sustained intermittently' by some of the cast, one reviewer commented.

Elizabeth died a spinster aged 73 on 30 September 1947 at Bradford Royal Infirmary. She left £82 in her will and the *Yorkshire Evening Post*, which published news of her death on the day of her demise, reported that she had begun her writing career as a schoolgirl aged 12 with a play on the Cinderella theme that she wrote for a Sunday school.

Few writers could claim to stand on a similar footing to the world-famous war poet Wilfred Owen, but this is exactly what poet and nurse Alberta Vickridge did. Alberta was born on 6 February 1890 in Bradford, to Albert and Edith Vickridge. Her father worked in the wool trade, importing wool from Ireland. During Alberta's early years, the family lived in Frizinghall and she and her sisters attended Bradford Girls' Grammar School, whose headmistress, Miss Roberts, encouraged her to forge a literary career. Miss Roberts was not the only one with faith in the young girl. On her 14th birthday, her parents paid for a book of her plays and poems to be printed and they presented her with a copy as her gift.

This confidence would prove well-founded, not only for Alberta's eventual achievements as a poet but she also later set up a small printing press in the attic of her house, from which she published the *Jongleur* poetry magazine for thirty years.

In 1924, she took first place in a poetry competition in the *Poetry Review*, in which her poem *Out of Conflict*, which told of her wartime experiences as a Voluntary Aid Detachment (VAD) nurse in Devon, relegated Wilfred Owen's entry to second place. She won a Bard's Crown and Bardic Chair at an eisteddfod in 1924 for her poem *The Foresaken Princess*, being the only Yorkshire woman to date to achieve such an honour.

HOLIDAY TIME

Bradford's holiday week took place in mid-August and was known locally as Bowling Tide. During this time, many workplaces closed entirely, meaning that everyone was off at the same time, so local attractions and public transport could be packed to capacity. For example, the *Yorkshire Post* of August 1928 reported with the headline 'start of great exodus to seaside', as around a fifth of the city's population left *en masse*, sometimes whole streets decamping to Scarborough or Blackpool, so that neighbours were literally next door on holiday too. Up to ninety trains a day would leave Bradford's stations (some departing as early as 5 a.m.) as Bowling Tide began, and there was even a dedicated 'Bradford boat' that left the port of Heysham for the Isle of Man.

Those who stayed closer to home didn't have to miss out on the fun, since Bowling Tide meant the possibility of visiting a travelling fair, the fair at Shipley Glen, or perhaps one of the parks such as Bowling or Peel Park. Another possibility was a charabanc trip. These open-top vehicles could seat around twenty passengers and arrived in Bradford around 1910, with services from firms including Kwick Transport Company of

Beckside Road in Lidget Green and Hirst Brothers of Dudley Hill. Among the favoured destinations for these jolly trips were rural towns and villages such as Skipton, Grassington and Ilkley. Even when wartime put paid to travel because of petrol restrictions, a Holidays at Home Week allowed people to focus on enjoying activities in their local area.

The first rail service reached Bradford on 1 July 1846, connecting the town to Leeds with hourly services, as well as offering direct services to places including Rugby, Derby and London. For journeys nearer to home, there were trams and buses, with the Corporation Motor Buses a familiar sight following their arrival in Bradford in 1926, initially offering a service between Bankfoot and Lister Park.

The Baildon gypsies

For centuries, the rural village of Baildon, five miles to the north of the city, was a location for gypsy fairs and weddings, with members of the Romany gypsy community coming from around the UK. The first gathering is recorded as early as 1770, and locals were always encouraged to take part, with crowds gathering not only for the fair, but also for gypsy weddings and the crowning of the gypsy kings.

There are early film recordings (available on YouTube) that show 1920's ceremonies with beautifully costumed gypsies watched by the crowds as couples pledged their troth or a new king was crowned.

SPORTS

From walking to cycling, football to tennis, the city has a fine tradition of sports for both sexes and as early as the 1920s, Lister's Mill had its own female football team. Although certain sports such as tennis and golf tended to be the province of wealthier women, perhaps because of the expense of the hobby, or simply social pressures, there were many opportunities to get active.

The earliest introduction to sport for most women would have been via the physical education provided through school. Many people have memories of this being a grim experience with sub-standard changing rooms, shabby swimming pools, and games lessons in the freezing cold. On a more pleasant note, many Bradfordians remember the annual Park Avenue sports day, organised by the Bradford Schools Athletic Association, which involved up to 3,000 children in massed displays of gymnastics and athletics.

On reaching adulthood, however, women were free to select their sport of choice and even in the Victorian age, the options were surprisingly wide. The recent enjoyment of the Tour de Yorkshire is no new fad. Since Victorian times, men and women have enjoyed cycling as a leisure pursuit. In the late 1800s, Eric S. Myers of Manningham Lane was offering 'new freedom' for women, allowing them to get out into the countryside on a bike. Other local makers included Ellis Briggs of Shipley and W.R. Baines of Thackley. Blaymire's Cycle Depot sold ladies' cycles from its Manchester Road depot and advertised 'private lessons in a covered riding school'.

Many women chose to enjoy the sport in the company of others, and clubs such as the Clarion Cycling Club (formed as a socialist leisure group) had a UK-wide membership, including a branch in Bradford, with members going as far afield as the Ribble Valley. In the early 1900s, the *Bradford Daily Telegraph* had a regular 'cycling gossip' column with news on club outings and events.

For example, on 13 July 1906, there was a report on Bradford Clarion Cycling Club's participation in a national annual competition where cyclists competed against a 'strong head wind'. Members stayed overnight in the Clarion Club House at Handforth in Cheshire, where it was reported that six 'of the stronger sex' of the Bradford group were forced to put up in a barn, which seems to confirm that women members were present. Also reported are the activities of Princeville Cycling Club and the Bradford Ladies' Cycling Club, who between them had visited locations including Ripon, Burnsall and Hardcastle Crags.

Rambling was another outdoor pursuit open to both men and women, and this was at the height of its popularity in the 1930s, the decade that the Kinder Trespass took place, as local newspapers carried itineraries and reports on the activities of different rambling groups around the country. For example, the *Leeds Mercury* of 1933 reported of a group meeting at 9.50 a.m. at Forster Square for members of the Bradford Corporation Tramways Rambling Club who walked on a 'heather ramble' over the moors, starting at Saltaire and ending at Ilkley.

Walking for ten miles or more would have been nothing out of the ordinary in the days before widespread car ownership. This was an age when people relished getting out into the fresh air after a week of manual labour or office work, most of which was probably spent in a noisy and indoor environment. A walk in any direction from the centre of Bradford could take a person out towards Shipley Glen, the starkly beautiful landscape leading towards Queensbury and Haworth, or perhaps the exhilarating views from somewhere such as Northcliffe Woods, with its views towards Bingley, Skipton and the Yorkshire Dales beyond.

A thousand miles in a thousand hours

One woman who took the walking craze to new heights was Emma Sharp of Laisterdyke who, in 1864, walked an incredible 1,000 miles in 1,000 hours, and is believed to have been the first woman to achieve this unusual feat.

Her epic challenge began on 17 September. However, rather than walking from one end of the country to the other, as might be expected from such a challenge nowadays, she simply walked half a mile in one direction and half a mile back the same way, taking thirty minutes for each way, watched by an excited crowd, who were shouting a mixture of encouragement and jeers of derision. She was reported to have brought a gun and her faithful dog with her to fend off attempts to put her off the challenge. Bets were riding on whether or not Emma would finish, and so there was a very real danger of interference.

Wearing what the *Bradford Observer* quaintly described as 'inexpressibles' – a pair of trousers – and a checked coat, she walked up and down by the Quarry Gap pub on Dick Lane, where her husband waited, apparently embarrassed by the fuss, according to his great-great-granddaughter in a newspaper report. He may have cringed at the fireworks display and hog roast put on to celebrate her triumphant finish.

For those who preferred indoor sport, the Dolphin Swimming Club has been going since 1888 and in its early days was famous for water polo. Many swimming pools were known as 'baths' in our period and some did exist within the same building as a bath house. Among the pools established at this time were Thornton Baths, Manningham Pool, Manchester Road and Wakefield Road. The Windsor Baths on Morley Street opened as Central Baths in 1905 offering swimming, baths, Turkish & Russian baths, and even ultra-violet ray treatments. The year 1915 saw the opening of the Lister Park open-air swimming pool with its diving board and springboard, and where 480 people could be seated for swimming galas.

Team sports

Many sports in the Victorian era would have been associated with men, such as golf, cricket and football. But they were also open to the women of Bradford. All-women sports clubs existed for cricket (with clubs at Lidget Green, Windhill and Bowling Old Lane) and golf – Northcliff Golf Club was well-known both in the area and further afield.

Rivalry between local towns could get quite heated. The *Yorkshire Evening Post* of March 1931 carried an appeal from the Bradford Women's Cricket League challenging the women of Leeds to send forward their best eleven. Their secretary Mr Metcalfe was quoted as saying:

> The Bradford girls' standpoint is this 'We can hit a hockey ball with a two-inch stick so what are we going to do with a bat four inches wide and 32 to 36 inches long. As for swimming and hockey, well what is to prevent us doing all three?'

This challenge came about after they'd heard that Leeds girls preferred swimming or hockey.

Saltaire was well-known for its gymnastics, and the world-famous Olympic gymnast Carrie Pollard trained and taught in the village. Carrie set up the Saltaire Ladies' Gymnastics Club in 1929, which was reportedly the first in the UK to train women in sports acrobatics. In 1948, four Saltaire gymnasts – Dorothy Hey, Audrey Rennard, Clarice Bell and Irene Hirst – represented Britain at the Olympics held in London, along with Bingley gymnast Dorothy Smith.

THEATRE, CINEMA AND DANCE

From at least the medieval age, Bradford had been visited by travelling players – jobbing actors and actresses who toured the country setting up shows wherever there was an audience, often on a market day when plenty of people were about. Darley Street and Market Street are both remembered in folk memory as such settings.

However, despite the popularity of such entertainment, from the start of the nineteenth century, the concept of going to see a show became more formalised. Historian Mr Scruton spoke of a permanent theatre in a barn on Southgate (now known as Sackville Street) as early as 1810, and one of the first plays in a permanent place in town was *The Siege of Bradford*, which was performed in the 1820s at a place on Market Street.

The year 1841 saw the opening of the Theatre Royal on Duke Street, which began under the name of the Liver Theatre and was well-established by the mid-nineteenth century. For twenty years it attracted many big names before it was eclipsed by a new playhouse on Manningham Lane, also known as the

Theatre Royal. Pullen's Music Hall, built in 1864, could seat 3,000 people on Brunswick Place, close to the modern-day Rawson Market.

Season tickets were offered for boxes at the original Theatre Royal, but only for people of 'acknowledged respectability'. For ordinary people the price was 6d in the gallery. Among the big names associated with this playhouse were Amy Sedgwick, Marie Jones and Julia St George. The latter had been fêted as the 'darling of the London stage' but, sadly, ended up in the workhouse in her old age, where she died after a fall at the age of 80. Another Theatre Royal regular was Mabel Sealby who, in 1905, during her stint as principal girl in that year's panto, prompted the future playwright J.B. Priestley (then aged around 11) to say: 'Every time she was mentioned in our local press, her named blazed out at me.'

The actors and actresses who appeared at Bradford theatres in the Victorian and Edwardian era were often very well-known to the public and enjoyed admiration and fame. Cigarette cards and postcards were produced showing flattering likenesses of these people, often dressed in theatrical costume.

A trip to theatre in its early years in Bradford was nothing like the polite experience it would become in the post-First World War years. To begin with, theatre-goers could be rowdy, a throwback to the type of antics associated with the audiences who pitched up to watch the travelling players. Notices were posted on theatre playbills of the Victorian age that stated that any audience member who was intoxicated, threw orange peel or nuts, or shouted out to the musicians or actors and actresses, would be 'instantly removed by the constables'.

These playbills provide a fascinating window into what was popular with audiences over the years. For example, in 1897, a bill for the People's Palace Theatre of Varieties on Manchester Road advertised a varied programme that included Flo Banks the electric spark dancer, Jessie Dover, who was a burlesque artiste and, last but not least, Professor Duncan's 'educated collie dogs'.

Bradford's best-known and well-loved theatre was the Alhambra, built in 1913 by music hall owner Francis Laidler. It opened to a specially-invited audience on 19 March 1914 by Mrs Francis Laidler, wife of the founder. 'The seating accommodation is for 1,800,' explained the *Leeds Mercury*, 'and hundreds more could have been accommodated if desired, but Mr Laidler has insisted that every person should have a plush-covered tip up seat and this has taken up more space.'

Five days later the Alhambra threw open its doors to the general public and a new chapter in the city's entertainment history began. First on the bill was a variety show that would run five days a week. Many women were among the performers, including 'principal boy' Alice Wyatt, Mamie Watson and Nellie Wallace – a Glasgow-born music hall star. These shows were staged twice a night and, after the First World War, Moss Empires Ltd joined forces with Laidler to source the top variety stars.

For many years, Francis Laidler's Sunbeams performed at the Alhambra. The Sunbeams were an all-girl dance and song group who were selected from the most talented children chosen at open audition. The girls were picked not only for their dance prowess but also for their looks – the wrong hairstyle could mean audition failure. Once in the group, however, the girls enjoyed the thrill of performing in Bradford, Leeds and sometimes further afield, and would be recognised in the street by keen theatre-goers. The girls had elocution lessons and, when out together, wore smart green overcoats, adding to their showbiz aura.

Laidler first used this girl group for Robin Hood at Princes Theatre in 1917. Sunbeams had to be aged at least 12 and in good health, with good school attendance. Many Sunbeams went on to enjoy a long career in showbusiness, including Pat Paterson, Mary O'Hare and Mamie Souter.

No piece on the city's theatre history would be complete without a look at St George's Hall, the UK's oldest music hall still in operation and the scene of many a rousing classical concert, thought-provoking lecture (Charles Dickens appeared here in

1854 to read scenes from *A Christmas Carol*), and protests, such as the suffragette protests (see Chapter 3). Opened on 29 August 1853, St Georges Hall was designed by Lockwood & Mawson, who went on to build the Town Hall and the Wool Exchange.

For many, it wasn't just about watching others tread the boards. There was a thriving amateur theatre and music scene. The Bradford Festival Choral Society was founded when St George's Hall opened, providing a massed choir of 200 singers. The group sang for Queen Victoria at Buckingham Palace in 1858.

Many Bradfordians have connections to, or have watched a play by, Bradford Catholic Players, an amateur dramatics group whose first show in 1927 *A Nautical Knot* was at St Joseph's Musical and Dramatical Society.

Three of Bradford's finest actresses

The city has produced many fine actresses over the years and the three spotlighted here are chosen because of their very different experiences.

Pat Paterson

Born at 15 Round Street, West Bowling, in 1910, Pat Paterson started her showbiz career as one of the afore-mentioned Sunbeams. Her mother Hannah (née Holroyd) was born in Bradford in 1880 and her father John Robb, a wool merchant, hailed from Kirkcaldy in Scotland.

Pat was one of three children and her mother encouraged her to take to the stage, paying for tap dancing and ballet classes and encouraging her to appear in local pantos. Like thousands of girls before her, Pat took a job in a textile mill when she left school. However, unlike her contemporaries, and with the blessing of her parents, she left her work in the velvet department at Lister's Mill behind at the age of 18 to try her luck in Hollywood.

By the age of 24, she was under contract to Fox film studios on a salary of £7,000 per year, an incredible sum at a time when a main household wage-earner back in the UK would be earning £100 a year.

Pat played the lead female role in *Charlie Chan Goes to Egypt* and she married French actor Charles Boyer. She returned to her home town several times, once appearing at the New Victoria Cinema, and also being treated to a civic reception, and signing autographs for fans.

Details of her films appeared in many local newspapers over the years, with her Yorkshire fans proudly watching her career progress. She died in 1978 in Phoenix, Arizona.

Gertie Millar

Gertie Millar was a girl from a mill community who went on to become a well-loved Edwardian actress and, eventually, Countess of Dudley. She was born on 21 February 1879 on Grimwith Street off Carlisle Road, and educated at Christ Church School. The Millar's home was close to the Theatre Royal, a place that inspired Gertie from a young age. Producer John Hart chose her to appear in his pantomime *Red Riding Hood* in the winter of 1891/92 and, the following year, the 13-year-old actress was appearing in a Manchester panto production.

Gertie began to make her name as a comic actress and, at the age of 14, joined the Arthur Brodgen Company for six years and then came back to Bradford before moving on to London and the *Cinderella* pantomime. By 1901, she was performing in the West End.

Gertie married composer Lionel Monckton and by 1916 had retired, although she returned to the Alhambra in Bradford to give her final performance in 1918. Gertie retained connections with her home town, giving to charities including the fledgling Bradford Royal Infirmary.

In 1924, Lionel died and, just two months later, Gertie married William Humble, the Second Earl of Dudley, whose family fortune came from coal and iron. She became Countess of Dudley and died at the age of 73 in 1952.

Caroline Marie Sudholme Lupton

Another Bradford actress was Caroline Marie Sudholme Lupton, born on 10 September 1875 at Hall Lane in Eccleshill and brought up in Baildon. Caroline had a middle-class upbringing. Her father Joseph was an auctioneer.

Caroline was a pupil at Salt's School and went on to help with the family auction business, before leaving to pursue a career on the stage. She moved to London, where she was employed at the Criterion Theatre, then appearing in West End productions and on stage in the US. She died in London in 1930, recognised as one of the most photographed beauties of the Edwardian era.

THE CINEMA AND DANCING

The cinema was a cheap and enjoyable night out, particularly in the days before television was more accessible to people. Like many large towns and cities, Bradford was home to numerous cinemas, ranging from large and luxurious concerns, like the Bradford Odeon, which opened in 1930 and could seat more than 3,300, through to smaller 'street corner' cinemas, where the same lady served you with tickets and sweets and then shone a torch down the aisle to guide you to your seats before returning at the interval with ice-creams.

The Bradford Odeon was quite highbrow in its 1930s heyday and had the London Symphony Orchestra playing at its opening gala. As cinemas competed for patrons, it was common for the managers of these establishments to secure big names to come along to the opening of a film or have a novelty guest such as a 'Wild West' horse for a Western.

Like the cinema, dance halls were a mainstay of social life and leisure and thousands of couples must have met at the cinema or dance hall over the years. One of the largest and most popular dance halls was Queen's Hall, part of the Windsor baths, built in 1914. Smaller venues, such as church halls and social clubs, also doubled as dance halls, providing much-needed income. For example, the Irish Club ran a Grand Irish

Ball in 1923, which ran from 7.30 p.m. to 1 a.m., with music from the Bradford Catholic Orchestra.

Refreshments, such as tea and biscuits, were available, or a bar serving alcohol in larger establishments. Getting ready to go out was part of the ritual, with girls visiting the hairdresser or doing each other's hair, making their own dresses or going out shopping, and saving up for high-heeled silver dance shoes.

Many girls liked to go along to dance lessons with a friend, so that they could practice in the privacy of a small class before braving a dance floor with a band or orchestra. In the 1870s, Professor Taylor ran lessons in Leeds and at Hanover Square in Bradford, promising 'thoroughly good' tuition, although what he was professor of isn't stated.

It was possible to book private tuition and some dance teachers taught both children and adults, teaching tap and ballet after school and older pupils in the early evening. Some classes would be accompanied by a piano and others by recorded music.

PAGEANTS AND ROYAL VISITS

Some of the most memorable moments in Bradford's history from the Victorian age onwards have been pageants and royal visits – high profile events that attracted crowds of thousands and were extensively reported and photographed in local and even national newspapers.

Being far from the seat of the British Royal Family in London, Bradford has perhaps received fewer high profile royal visits than other cities of a similar size. For example, despite there being a Queen Victoria statue in Bradford (outside the Media Museum), Victoria never actually visited, although many people will have travelled to Leeds to witness her trip there on 7 September 1858, when she opened Leeds Town Hall.

The lack of the queen's presence in Bradford didn't deter the public from enthusiastically embracing Victoria's diamond jubilee celebrations in 1897, when Bradford was elevated to city status to mark the occasion, alongside Hull and Nottingham.

The diamond jubilee was marked with public celebrations on 22 June. Sixty thousand medals were distributed to Sunday schools, made by Bradford jeweller Fattorini. On the morning of the celebrations, 3,000 children were given a 'substantial breakfast' by volunteers from the Cinderella Club.

This jubilee also saw an exciting first for Bradfordians when some of the first film of the jubilee celebrations in London the previous day were brought to Bradford by train and shown to crowds of 10,000 in one weekend. Bradford man James Appleton organised the film show, and the film was so 'hot off the press' that it had been developed on the train during the journey between London and Bradford Forster Square.

There was also a gun salute at noon in Lister Park by the West Riding Yorkshire Artillery Volunteers, which was timed to coincide with the arrival of Queen Victoria at St Paul's Cathedral in London for her thanksgiving service.

The town hall was decorated with flags, streamers and bunting, as were the markets and Forster Square, and the Lister, Peel, Horton and Bradford Moor parks. Peals of bells rang from the town hall throughout the day, adding to the celebratory atmosphere.

The procession must have been a wonderful sight as crowds pushed forward to watch a display that included mounted police and fire brigades belonging to various mills including Whetley and Britannia. On that day there was a fairground at Peel Park and a balloon ascent was promised by Mr Reuben Bramhall of Bradford. There were performances by mill bands and dancing until 9.15 p.m. The balloon ascent was much remarked upon in the local press, and Mr Bramhall was still making flights over the city two years later. This time, Mr Bramhall got as far as Clitheroe Golf Links, travelling forty-two miles in seventy minutes. Such flights were popular events, reported as early as the 1870s in the district.

The programme for the jubilee promised:

> ... at dusk the town hall will be brilliantly illuminated with globed gas jets made to a special design ... a

searchlight will be manipulated from the tower of the Town Hall, changing with six coloured lights.

All traffic except trams were stopped and other points around the city were lit up.

Three huge bonfires were lit at Wrose Hill, Horton Bank Top and Allerton, part of a chain of a hundred around Yorkshire. As the crowds dispersed at the end of the day, talk was of the fun that had been had and sights that had been seen – a day in the city that would be talked about for years to come. Decades later, grandparents told their children 'I was there'.

Five years earlier at a much more formal occasion, Victoria's son the Prince of Wales (the future Edward VII) and his wife Princess Alexandra paid a visit to Saltaire as guests of Titus Salt, staying at his Milner Field mansion. They opened Saltaire's new technical school, built at cost of £30,000. 'Triumphal arches' were erected along the route between Lister Park and Saltaire, which the local press trumpeted as 'hundreds of flags and banners and Venetian masts with pennons gay'.

In the carriages accompanying the prince and princess were the High Sheriff of Yorkshire (Sir Henry D. Ingilby) and Lady Ingilby, the Lord Lieutenant (Earl Fitzwilliam) and Countess Fitzwilliam, the Earl and Countess of Bective and Lady Olivia Taylour, Lieutenant-Colonel Clarke, Lady Suffield, the Honourable and Reverend P. Yorke Savile, Sir Philip Cunliffe-Owen, Mr Christopher Sykes MP, Mr and Mrs Titus Salt, Mr and Mrs Edward Salt, Mr George Salt, Mr Charles Stead (chairman of the Shipley local board), and Mrs and Miss Stead.

King George V and Queen Mary visited Bradford, Shipley and Saltaire in 1918 as part of a tour of northern cities. The sentiments of this visit were echoed in a visit by George VI and Queen Elizabeth in 1937, visiting the 'industrial north'. On the couple's second visit, there was a military band and guard of honour at the town hall. A film in the Yorkshire Film Archive shows the crowd craning their necks to see the royals. The queen stood with the lord mayor's wife and was presented with a bouquet by a Miss Joan Riley.

The Great Bradford Exhibition of 1904

One of the city's greatest ever community events was the Great Bradford Exhibition, which ran for several months in Lister Park and was opened by the Prince and Princess of Wales.

Thousands watched the parade, with the royals in an open-top carriage travelling to launch the exhibition at Lister Park on 4 May 1904. The procession headed up Darley Street and along Manningham Lane, where the royal couple were met by the mayor at Cartwright Hall, and the prince unveiled a plaque.

Amy Wade, granddaughter of the mayor, was chosen to present a bouquet to the princess and she herself received a doll as a present. The *Yorkshire Post* said she wore 'a charming dress of ivory soft silk, trimmed with three flounces of rich embroidered silk lace ...' designed by Mrs Warren of the Royal Arcade in Bradford.

Original documents and memorabilia from the exhibition show that it was organised on a grand scale with exhibits for a wide range of ages and interests. Among the quirky attractions were a model hospital, Somali village, a large water chute and a switchback railway (early roller-coaster). Dressmaking demonstrations were staged regularly and visitors were invited to make their way around a palace of illusions.

Somali village

These days this would be known as a 'pop-up' village. Somalians actually lived in this village for the run-up to the exhibition, where there would have been full-sized huts, kitchens and gardens.

Even at this event, the values of the bygone Victorian age were still in evidence, with first-class and second-class teas. The programme shows that the patronesses of the women's society included two duchesses, seven countesses and eleven ladies, as well as Mrs Titus Salt, who was on the executive committee, and Dr Charlotte Hodgins.

The women's section was very much aimed at the role of females in the home and as nurturers, with arts and crafts, education and domestic skills. Students from local schools and colleges did demonstrations such as cooking, laundry, needlework, housewifery and physical training, while adverts in the programme included advice on health from Madam Zara Lee from Philadelphia who, working from premises at Manchester Road and Marshfield Street, could 'character read from photographs' and was a scientific palmist and phrenologist.

Continuing the female stereotyping typical of this age, the model hospital was fitted out to show the domestic and medical side of home nursing, and the working and practical value of a day nursery for children whose parents worked.

Although education and personal betterment were catered for, there were plenty of thrills and fun too. Adverts for the water chute claimed that 'the absolute safety of the lightning-paced ride with its exciting dash into the water and after flight into space makes this exercise both exhilarating and enjoyable'. And in the evening the park was transformed by lights from coloured lamps and Chinese lanterns, making it a 'veritable trip to fairyland'. In a world where few houses were lit by electricity, this would genuinely have brightened up people's lives and those lucky enough to hold season tickets must have returned many times.

The Saltaire Exhibition

Exhibition Road in Saltaire is named after the large-scale Royal Yorkshire Jubilee Exhibition held in the village, which was opened by Princess Beatrice on 6 May 1887. The five-month long event was centred upon a new exhibition building that cost £12,000. Exhibition-goers paid a shilling entry and then could have access to a range of attractions, including a toboggan run, working dairy, maze and Japanese village. One of the most memorable attractions was an inland lighthouse, which beamed its light across Saltaire and the surrounding countryside each evening.

Attendees on 24 June had a more exciting time than most when a lion-taming demonstration by a Major Rowe went wrong due to what the *Nottingham Times* called a lioness in a 'bad temper' who knocked Rowe to the floor and tore his coat from top to bottom. He managed to recover his composure, run past the six lions and exit the cage, only to bravely return later that evening for a repeat performance, which went more smoothly.

During the exhibition's run cheap excursion trains ran, bringing in the public from as far afield as Oldham, York, Scarborough and Nottingham, and helping to boost visitor numbers, which reached more than 800,000.

Bradford Pageant

The Bradford Pageant was another big day in the life of the city and one which, because it involved hundreds of schoolchildren, lives on in family folklore for many. The outdoor event ran from 13 to 18 July 1931 and was part of a huge programme of historical pageants that were so popular in the first half of the twentieth century, being staged in towns and villages from Cornwall to the far north of Scotland.

Bradford's historical pageant featured eighty horses and 7,500 performers who, incredibly, outnumbered the audience of 4,000. The pageant told 'the living story of Bradford's glory' and coincided with a wool fair staged for the 600th anniversary of the introduction of wool-weaving to England by Flemish weavers.

Frank Lascelles was the pageant master and lived up to the title, having staged other spectaculars in towns including Oxford and Carlisle. The show opened in the year 71AD in a Brigantes village, then ran through the medieval era, the growth of the woollen trade and the Civil War.

> There is both accuracy and breadth of treatment in the scene representing the resentment of the workers against the new inventions that were to end the hand combing and hand weaving jobs. (Bradford Observer)

In 1947, a post-war fair with a forward thinking 'Bradford makes it' motto was held, which had a hall of fashion and fabric to show West Riding fabrics made into clothes. Twenty-six wire models were dressed to show Bradford's taste, design and knowledge in the whole art of turning their many and world-famous fabrics into gowns, coats and costumes for the 'woman of today'.

CHAPTER ELEVEN

In the Footsteps of Bradford's Women

✦

Although the scope of this book reaches through to 1950, the legacy of Bradford's women continues into the present day. The 1950s are still well within living memory and the city is home to the descendants of many of the remarkable women whose lives we've discovered throughout the previous chapters.

Although the city looks very different to how it would have been at the start of our period, someone from the mid- to late-nineteenth century might still recognise the city without too much a stretch of imagination. Thoroughfares, such as Ivegate, Market Street and Darley Street, are still in existence, and well-known Victorian public buildings, such as St George's Hall and City Hall, have changed little over the decades and still play their part in civic and public life.

In the suburbs, new housing estates and industrial complexes stand where there were once textile mills and row upon row of workers' housing. But it's still possible to glimpse into bygone Bradford through the remaining pubs, shops and places of worship that were part of the lives of Bradford women in decades gone by.

LANDMARKS

Between 1850 and 1875, the town made up for its lack of striking public buildings as new landmarks were created, underlining

Bradford's status as a prosperous textile centre. In this quarter of a century the town hall, St George's Hall, the Mechanics' Institute and the Wool Exchange were all built in the centre of town. Each is still in existence, although the Wool Exchange no longer rings to the sound of traders greeting each other and bartering their wares, but to the quiet murmur of book buyers and the hiss of the coffee machine.

City Hall

City Hall, popularly known to generations of Bradfordians as the town hall, has been at the centre of life in Bradford since the Victorian era. Royal parades, heated protests, impassioned speeches and civic celebrations have all been staged here over the decades. Now the town hall is at the centre of the attractive Centenary Square, which boasts the country's largest man-made water feature in a city centre.

The town hall was designed by Lockwood & Mawson architects, who also designed the nearby Wool Exchange and the textile mill at Saltaire. A section of the building houses the Bradford Police Museum, which looks at the history of policing and crime & punishment from the nineteenth century onwards. Keep a look out for occasional guided tours and open days at the town hall.

City Hall, Centenary Square, Bradford BD1 1HY tel: 01274 433678 (tourist information centre); website: www.visitbradford.com

Lister's Mill

Once the world's largest silk factory, Lister's Mill dominates the skyline and has been a landmark since its completion more than 150 years ago. Today, the restored building has been converted into apartments and offices and, at the time of writing, visitors can drop in to the community centre and café to see the interior of the building.

Lister Mills, Lilycroft Road, Manningham, Bradford BD9 5BD

World Heritage village of Saltaire

Bradford's World Heritage village Saltaire played a key role in textile history when a 'model village' was established here by Titus Salt, opening on 20 September 1853. Today's visitors can see the houses where the workers, overlookers and mill-managers lived, explore Salt's Mill – the heart of Salt's textile empire – and visit many of the facilities he provided for the workers, including a church, railway station, meeting hall and park.

Saltaire Tourist Information, Salts Mill, Victoria Road, Saltaire BD18 3LA tel: 01274 437942 village website: www.saltairevillage. info

Bradford Industrial Museum

Since 1974, Bradford Industrial Museum has existed as a museum within a mill, celebrating the city's role in the textile trade. The former Moorside Mill still retains a large collection of mill machinery, as well as transport artefacts from the city's history, including buses, trams, cars, vans and lorries.

There are also mill-workers' terraced houses, which have been decorated and furnished to reflect different styles from the Victorian era through to the 1970s.

Moorside Mills, Moorside Road, Eccleshill, Bradford BD2 3HP tel: 01274 435900 website: www.bradfordmuseums.org/venues/ bradford-industrial-museum

Cartwright Hall and Lister Park

Lister Park, named after textile baron Samuel Cunliffe Lister, who built nearby Lister's Mill, was the venue for the 1904 Bradford Exhibition. The park has statues of Samuel Lister and Titus Salt, and a Norman arch, created for the visit of the Prince and Princess of Wales in 1882.

Within the grounds stands Cartwright Hall, the city's art gallery, which was opened in 1904 after Samuel Cunliffe Lister gifted £40,000 to the city.

Lister Park, Park Road, Bradford BD9 4NR tel: 01274 431000 website: http://www.bradforddistrictparks.org/sites/parks/parks. php?ID=41

St George's Hall

Reportedly the UK's oldest concert hall still in use, St George's Hall opened on 29 August 1853 and was designed by Lockwood & Mawson.

During its 150-year history, the hall has played host to hundreds of concerts, plays and amateur theatricals and was also one of the venues that formed part of the opening ceremony for the village of Saltaire.

The concert hall has a busy programme of events throughout the year, including concerts, amateur dramatics, orchestral performances and dance shows. At the time of writing, St George's Hall was closed for renovation, and is due to reopen during 2019.

St George's Hall, Bridge Street, Bradford BD1 1JT tel: 01274 432375 website: www.bradford-theatres.co.uk

Bradford Cathedral

Often overlooked as a historic building and visitor attraction because of its location, slightly out of town, Bradford Cathedral was built in the early fifteenth century on the site of a much older building. This has been a site of Christian worship since around 627AD and was a parish church until 1919.

The building played an interesting role in the Civil War, when its towers were hung with wool sacks to protect it against royalist artillery attacks.

Visitors are welcome to explore the building and to enjoy the regular art exhibition and music performances, as well as take part in daily worship.

Bradford Cathedral, 1 Stott Hill, Bradford BD1 4EH tel: 01274 777720 website: www.bradfordcathedral.org

Undercliffe Cemetery

A very special site in Bradford's history, Undercliffe Cemetery is a Victorian burial ground that provides a snapshot of the best of Victorian funerary art, with some beautiful gravestones with unusual carvings relating to the trade or interests of the deceased; as well as huge mausoleums for some of Bradford's wealthiest and most influential families.

Talks and tours are held for groups and schools, and volunteers help maintain the burial site and monuments. You can download an interactive trail from the website.

Undercliffe Cemetery, 127 Undercliffe Lane, Bradford BD3 0QD tel: 01274 642276 email: undercliffecemetery@hotmail.co.uk website: www.undercliffecemetery.co.uk

Little Germany

A unique area of the city, which is where German settlers traded after arriving here in the 1850s. Fifty-five of the district's eighty-five buildings are categorised as listed buildings, and it's possible to get a sense of the importance of the wool trade with the warehouses, offices and showrooms built to impress wool trade clients and underline the importance of trade to the city.

Little Germany, Bradford BD1 5RW tel: 01274 433678 (tourist information centre) website: www.visitbradford.com

WALKING TRAILS

Bradford City Centre Heritage Trail

Explore more than thirty city sites on this walking trail of the core of Bradford, which starts from City Hall and follows a two-hour trail, which can be shortened if required. Among the highlights are Ivegate, one of the city's oldest streets, which still retains a medieval look, the many buildings of Little Germany, and the area around the Midland Hotel, once the hub of the town where dozens of trains arrived and departed each day.

Bradford Peace Trail

The Bradford Peace Trail takes a look at the people and organisations who have made a difference to life in the city over the years as a self-guided walking tour. The women featured include Florence White, Miriam Lord, Margaret McMillan, and a plaque for the Bradford Women's Humanity League.

Download here: https://routestopeace.files.wordpress.com/2013/02/rtp-trail-booklet-web-corrected.pdf

Manningham walk

Enjoy a self-guided walk around the historic Manningham district, home to landmarks such as Lister's Mill, Cartwright Hall and the Bradford Children's Hospital. Bradford Libraries' walk leaflet can be found online at http://bradfordjewish.org.uk/wp-content/uploads/2013/04/Manningham-History-Walk-Leaflet.pdf and includes fourteen different landmarks, recounting the district's history from Saxon times onwards.

Bradford Jewish Heritage Trail

Follow in the footsteps of Bradford's Jewish community on this self-guided trail, which centres around Manningham Lane, Queen's Road and Lister Park, as well as the Spring Gardens and Bowland Street synagogues. Download at the Bradford Jewish website: http://bradfordjewish.org.uk/900-2/

ARCHIVES

Discover more about Bradford's women at these libraries and archives.

Bradford Archives

Part of the West Yorkshire Archive Service group, Bradford Archives is located in the same building as the Bradford Local Studies Library in the centre of Bradford. Here you can explore hundreds of years-worth of historical documents and photographs charting life in Bradford. There are biographies, programmes from events such as theatre performances and bazaars, diaries, papers of local businesses, church, school and poor law records, and council papers.

You'll need to bring ID and proof of address for your first visit, and booking is advised to ensure space at one of the tables.

Bradford Archives, Central Library, Princes Way, Bradford BD1 1NN tel: 01274 435099 email: Bradford@wyjs.org.uk website: www.wyjs.org.uk/archives

Bradford Local Studies Library

Located within Bradford Central Library, the Bradford Local Studies Library is home to thousands of items relating to the city's history, geography, architecture and heritage, including books, manuscripts, microfilm, oral histories and photographs.

Both an online index and a card index give access to different items within the collection, and there are seventeen public computers. There are more than 2,000 bound volumes of historic local newspapers, as well as over 6,000 books for borrowing and/or reference.

Bradford Local Studies Library, Old Central Library, Prince's Way, Bradford BD1 1NN tel: 01274 433688 website: https://www.bradford.gov.uk/libraries/find-your-local-library/local-studies-library/

SPECIAL COLLECTIONS

With more than a hundred collections of books and papers relating to the history of Bradford, Bradford University and Yorkshire, Special Collections is a unique place to study Bradford's past. The best-known collection is the J.B. Priestley Archive, with plays, theatre programmes and press cuttings, and there are also collections on textiles and dyeing, the daybook of Titus Salt, and family letters relating to Sir Isaac Holden.

J B Priestley Library, University of Bradford, BD7 1SR tel: 01274 233301 email: special-collections@bradford.ac.uk website: www.bradford.ac.uk/library/special-collection

Thornton Antiquarians Society archives

A small, private archive open to the public by appointment. The archive is cared for by Thornton Antiquarian Society as part of the South Square project. Material includes oral histories, books by and about Thornton people, photographs, maps and artefacts.

South Square, Thornton, Bradford BD13 3LD tel: 01274 834747 email: info@southsquarecentre.co.uk website: www. southsquarecentre.co.uk

The Saltaire Archive

A unique archive relating to the history of Saltaire, from the original planning of the model village through to the present day. Public exhibitions of some of the material are held regularly, and selected materials are displayed in Salt's Mill. Visitors are welcome to make an appointment to view the material, which includes photographs, newspaper reports, Salt's family papers, diaries, souvenir guides, television documentaries, films and personal memory files.

Saltaire Archive, Shipley College, Victoria Road, Shipley BD18 3LQ email: saltairestories@gmail.com website: www.shipley. ac.uk/studying-in-saltaire/saltaire-archive

Author's note

A woman of Bradford who lived through the years 1850 to 1950 would have seen huge changes on both a national and a local scale. The upheaval of the Industrial Revolution, changes in education for both women and men, the fight for the vote and the horror of two world wars, changed both the UK and the city forever.

And yet more change was still to come. As we now know, with the benefit of hindsight, there would be many more battles for women to fight and plenty of struggles ahead, with the social changes of the 'Swinging Sixties', more widespread employment of married women in the workplace, and the challenges posed by large-scale immigration into the city with the arrival of a new group of incomers from Asia and the Caribbean.

But as the old saying goes, the more things change, the more they stay the same. I feel that those women of early Victorian Bradford might not find the city so greatly changed today. Our people are friendly and welcoming, we face change with determination and Yorkshire grit and look ahead to the future, whatever it might hold.

Photo Captions

01 - Textile mills dominated the skyline at the height of the textile trade © Tim Green

02 - Heaton Mount, once a grand family home in Manningham and now part of the University of Bradford © Tim Green

03 - Kirkgate Market, a favourite with generations of shoppers © Judy Barrett

04 - Cockle Sarah © Bradford Museums & Galleries

05 - Wealthy girls were largely taught at home in the nineteenth century © British Library Flickr

06 - Statue of W.E. Forster © Tim Green

07 - English Heritage plaque commemorating Rachel and Margaret McMillan at their lodging place on Tweedy Road, Bromley © Open Plaques

08 - Saltaire Institute © Tim Green

09 - Brooch in the suffragette colours of white, purple and green © Glasgow Women's Library

10 - 1911 Suffragette procession in London © Library of Congress, George Bain Collection

11 - Shipley Glen, scene of a mass votes for women rally in 1908 © Tuck D B Postcards

12 - Suffragette placard procession, © Library of Congress, George Bain Collection

13 - Barbara Castle pictured in 1965 © National Archives of Malawi

14 - National Spinsters' Association campaigners © West Yorkshire Archive Service, Bradford

15 - Bradford Town Hall, the seat of office of the city's lord mayor and lady mayoress © Tuck D B Postcards

16 - An Edwardian postcard celebrating Bradford's beautiful women © Tuck D B Postcards

17 - Once women had children they were often out of the workforce (Author's Collection)

18 - Novels such as Charles Dickens' *Oliver Twist* portrayed the workhouse as a place to be feared © British Library Flickr

19 - The Holme on Thornton Road, built in 1798 and reputedly Bradford's first factory © British Library Flickr

20 - The chimney at Lister's Mill. Generations of Bradford people have grown up hearing the tale that the top of the chimney was wide enough to take a horse and cart © Tim Green

21 - Plaque commemorating the Manningham Mills Strike of 1890-91 © Tim Green

22 - Salt's Mill, once a village at the heart of Bradford's textile industry and now a World Heritage Site © Tim Green

23 - Memorial to those killed in the Newlands Mill disaster © Tim Green

24 - Bradford Forster Square, the first sight of Bradford for immigrants arriving in the city by train © Tuck D B Postcards

25 - Drawing of migrants arriving by ship after a long and crowded sea journey © British Library Flickr

26 - Australian poster inviting people to start a new life in a new country © Library of Congress

27 - Poster for the Division for Foreign Born Women, which supported female US immigrants © Library of Congress

28 - Nurse Mitchell, matron of Sir Titus Salt Hospital in the First World War © *Shipley at War*

29 - Women's canteen at Phoenix Works, Bradford – painting by Flora Lion © Imperial War Museums

30 - Low Moor Ironworks (Author's Collection)

31 - Peel Park pictured in 1916 (Author's Collection)

32 - Allerton's war memorial is relatively unusual in featuring a female figure © Tim Green

33 - Crowds at Bowling Tide, early twentieth century © East Bowling History Group

34 - Bowling Park in 1916 © Tuck D B Postcards

35 - Edwardian theatre star Gertie Millar (Author's Collection)

36 - Scene from the 1931 Bradford Pageant (Author's Collection)

37 - City Hall © Tim Green

38 - Bradford cathedral: Bradford Cathedral © Tim Green

Index